In *Confluence*, Douglas Henning offers a fascinating fusion of Buddhism, Christianity and psychology. Regardless of your familiarity with the subjects, as you read you will have a new appreciation for their shared wisdom. I will be pondering how to put what I've learned into practice in the coming days. I'm so glad I didn't pass this one up!

—Chris S. Baker, author of The Invitation: How Open and Relational Theology Enhances N.T. Wright's Use of Vocation in Atonement

A warmly readable blend of storytelling, humor, and hard-won wisdom, this book weaves together the teachings of Jesus, Buddha, and psychology into a compelling case that helping others—especially the least among us—is the deepest purpose of human life. Henning's honest, narrative-driven approach will both delight and quietly convict readers who find it easier to retreat into ideas than into the messier, more demanding work of genuine presence and relationship.

—Tim Miller, DThM, author of The Silence of the Lamb: Exploring the Hiddenness of Christ and God

Douglas Henning brings a diverse background to his work on this topic. Born from the inner work of questioning, doubting, and searching, Henning's journey brought him out of the comfortable, dominating past, through the currents of his military overseas experience, and into the world of Buddhist mindfulness. Henning seems to have landed, as the title states, at the confluence of wisdom drawn from authentic Christian faith (life and teachings of Jesus Christ), Buddhism, and grounded in his own studies in psychology. Throughout the read, Henning's passionate attraction for locating a sense of well-being exposed the intersection of Buddhist practices and the life and teachings of Jesus. Henning posits a Buddhist influence on Jesus, "Buddhism which was present for at least a couple of centuries before Jesus' family living there as refugees in Egypt", which he suggests strengthens Jesus' message. Consistent with open and relational theology, Henning's conclusions ultimately lead to being present in the now of life and living. Filtering that message through the lens of modern theories in psychology. Henning suggests, "Living in the present is a principle shared by Buddhism, Christianity, and psychology."

Confluence is a relevant read for all students of faith or even non-faith who are on their own journey toward wisdom. This book certainly has its place on the shelf of serious students, teachers, pastors, chaplains, and spiritual practitioners.

—Tracy L Tucker, ThD, BCC, CT, author of Can We
Talk About Death? An Open and Relational Vision

Raised in Christian fundamentalism, shaped by an unexpected encounter with Buddhism during the Vietnam War, and formed professionally as a psychologist and therapist, Doug Henning has lived his way into a rare kind of wisdom. In this richly observed spiritual autobiography, he traces how these three traditions—rather than competing or tearing him apart—have deepened and illuminated one another across a fully lived life. Henning's storytelling is both honest and inviting, and his hard-won insight that Jesus, Buddha, and psychology are more confluence than contradiction will resonate with anyone who has ever felt pulled between belief systems. Readers may find themselves, as more than one reviewer has, imagining the spiritual autobiography they might write—and smiling at the permission this book quietly gives them to live in more than one truth at once.

—Donald Heinz, professor of Religious Studies,
a Christian social-ethicist, minister

In this thoughtful, deeply personal book, the author uses both autobiography and scholarship to draw meaning from his lifelong journey as a student of wisdom in Christianity, psychology, and Buddhism. The author approaches all three of these traditions with curiosity, humility, and a desire for shared understanding. In a time when religious differences too often produce suspicion or fear rather than dialogue, this book reminds us of the need to establish common ground for the common good. Whether or not the reader agrees with every hypothesis and proposal here, this book contributes in a meaningful way to the urgent work of interreligious bridge-building. This book encourages us all to listen closely to our neighbors' wisdom while remaining rooted in the wisdom of our own traditions. In the end, the author's story is not presented as a final answer but as a roadmap which was useful to him, marked by many signposts along the way. I am grateful that the author has shared his spiritual journey so openly with the rest of us.

—Mark Hayse, Ph.D. Director, Mabee Library,
MidAmerica Nazarene University

Confluence

Integrated Wisdom from
Jesus, Buddha & Psychology

AN INTRODUCTION

DOUGLAS HENNING, PhD

Paperback: 978-1-968136-54-3
Ebook: 978-1-968136-53-6

Printed in the United States of America

Library of Congress Cataloguing-in-Publication Data
Confluence: Integrated Wisdom of Jesus, Buddha & Psychology An Introduction /
Douglas Henning

To the students and clients of fifty years, who showed me what good psychology actually looks like, one life at a time.

Table of Contents

CHAPTERS   **PAGE**

Introduction   1

PART I

Introduction   11   My Background and the book's
                             rationale

One   17   **Back Stories** - Relevant Background
                             of Psychological theories,
                             Developmentalism, Religions, & the
                             author

Two   29   **Developmental Model of Faith** -
                             Psychology, and The Self

Three   43   **Integrative Wisdom** - Thinking
                             Confluenltly

PART II

Four   57   **Buddha Instructs My Christian Faith** - He Restores My Faith

Five   63   **Four Truths of Buddhism -** Impermanence, Change is Constant, Fallibility of Memory, Attributions, and Essence, Co-Arising

Six   81   **Early Influences: Buddha and Jesus** - Integrating Wisdoms with Psychology

Seven   93   **Doctrines and Worldly Convention**

Eight   107   **Problems with Words and Concepts**

Nine   117   **Concluding Thoughts: A Tapestry**

About the Author   127

Acknowledgements 129

Preface

In writing this, as I have in many of my writings over the last several decades, I help myself understand my own beliefs more deeply. This is akin to coming to a better understanding of things after you have taught them. Much of my life, at various times, I've struggled or questioned different aspects of my Christian faith. At least part of the reason this was a struggle was the conservative and fundamentalist environment in which I was raised. This environment, for the most part, was not open to questions about its fundamental doctrines, such as the basic tenets of Christianity, or its daily rituals. Questioning these out loud was taboo and equal to heresy. It was an us-and-them, with them being anyone whose beliefs differed from ours. So if I rejected the beliefs of the Southern Baptist church, I was a traitor, or worse, I was left with nothing. And nothing felt much too empty.

This was similar to being on a road trip and finding that a flood had washed out the bridge on the road you were traveling on. Foolishly thinking that you had to stop and not continue. No other version of Christianity was an option. To Southern Baptists, Catholics were not Christian, and Mormonism was a cult. So those were not an option; liberal Christian denominations, like Lutheran and Episcopalian, were just social gospels, which weren't authentically Christian either. Unitarianism wasn't even a consideration, much like Judaism, Muslim, and Buddhism. But in reality, I've come to believe over the last many decades that there are actually many alternate routes in the universe of spirituality. These aren't just second-best roads, like a detour over an unpaved roadway around the washed-out bridge. The alternate route turns out to be beautiful and reaches the same destination. So when a roadblock occurs on a Christian path, and one shifts to a more psychological path to wisdom and insight, they can still reach the ultimate knowing, or wisdom. Or, within the context of this book, a Buddhist path will also lead to ultimate enlightenment. No need for panic, just be patient with the new route.

Roadblocks in our spiritual journey can take many forms: cultural limitations, blemished models we had been led to believe were authentic, and more sophisticated knowledge that disproves the logic of our simple views, to name a few. Culture-specific limitations might include behaviors deemed evidence of sincere faith in one society but not in another, such as eating certain foods or drinking alcohol, or behaviors like going to movies. Blemished models, such as a protestant pastor, Catholic priest, or Muslim Imam, that we discover have a secret part of their life which comes to light and is the reason a person gives for no longer believing. The sophisticated versus the unsophisticated level of knowledge, such as scientific wisdom about evolution, as opposed to a Sunday School lesson from the book of Genesis about the creation of the earth.

As I matured, I began attending a Christian college at the age of nineteen. The college was a different denomination, Anglican, from my religious roots, which were Southern Baptist and Calvinist. I noticed that fellow students believed different doctrines from the ones I had been raised with. An example of the two differences, which seemed significant at the time, was that Baptists believed that once you were saved, that was it—once *saved, always saved*. Anglicans thought that a person could lose their salvation by rejecting the Holy Spirit and saying they no longer believed in God. Also, that merely getting saved was just the first step toward a deeper spiritual life. The second step was getting *entirely sanctified*. I don't remember being too disturbed by these differences. Probably because they appeared to be Christian, like I was, this marked the beginning of realizing there were different points of view within Christianity. This was also the beginning of my questioning various aspects of my faith, a process that would continue throughout my life. In most cases, as I formulated these questions in my mind, I voiced these doubts only to those closest to me. A typical pattern of this doubting was to hold certain inconsistencies in suspension, while I searched for and waited for more confirming or disconfirming data.

I was first exposed to Buddhism and Buddhists in the late 1960s during the Vietnam War while stationed in Udorn Royal Thai Air Force Base, Thailand. The Air Base was just outside Udon Thani in the Northeast corner of Thailand, forty miles from Vientiane, Laos. I worked the night shift on the F-4 Phantom jet aircraft. Because the barracks had only screen external walls and no air conditioning, sleeping during the day in humid Southeast Asia was, to say the least, very difficult. Since I could only sleep a few hours during the day, I spent my days working out at the gym, teaching conversational English at a local trade school, visiting an orphanage for Thai-American babies, and visiting a Christian hospitality house in town. This year, as a twenty-three-year-old, impacted me in ways that I only came to understand many years later. At the time, what impressed me the most was the gentleness and kindness of the people of Thailand. I had been raised Southern Baptist in Eastern

Kentucky and was in church every time the door opened. Being Christian and being in church was just what I learned to do, a lifestyle. While attending a Christian service early in my time at Udorn, I came to faith as an adult. Over the year in Thailand, I came to appreciate and admire the people and their Buddhist culture.

To add to the several dynamics that were occurring in my personal life, my wife Joyce was home in Oregon and pregnant. I'd go home to her, who had gone through a pregnancy, become a mother, and meet my three-month-old son. Obviously, I had a lot on my mind. In many ways, I could relate to the father in the movie *Old Yeller*, set in post-Civil War Texas. In the movie, the dad has to leave home during the summer on a cattle drive, and leaves his wife and young son, about 12 years old, to fend for themselves on their homestead. Soon after the dad leaves, a stray yellow dog shows up, which the boy and his mom take in. The dog and the boy become inseparable as the dog takes on and scares off a series of intruders and predators, like raccoons, snakes, and bears. Toward the end of the story, before the dad returns, the dog defends the boy by fighting an intruder with rabies. As a result, the dog comes down with rabies, foaming at the mouth, and so on. Thus, the boy must put the dog down by shooting it. When the dad gets home, the viewers realize that the dad can't relate to what his son and wife have gone through, as his son has come of age, essentially become a man. I had a lot to adjust to, in addition to sorting out what it was like to be in a war.

I'm still not totally clear on the specifics of Buddhism's role, due to this process being largely subconscious, in my adjustment to being home, and navigating my mid-adult years. What I have been aware of is being drawn to Buddhism, even if I wasn't sure how to pursue it. I do recall specifically admitting later in my adult years that if I were choosing a religion as a middle-aged professor and psychologist, I'd have to give Buddhism a lot of consideration.

Private Thoughts

As an adult, because I worked in and attended church in conservative Christian circles, I knew if I were frank about some of my doubts with people in those social circles, I would have lost friends. At least this is what I assumed. I expected this to be especially true with those people with whom I worked. Admitting this here, I can see how that might have been seen as somewhat hypocritical. I realize that my silence, to a certain extent, allowed others to assume things about me that were not entirely true. For example, a student told me once that she felt betrayed because I had voiced acceptance, even approval, of my son, his wife, and her family, who are Muslim. This came in response to a Muslim guest speaker I had invited to class who wore a hijab. The class was a graduate course on multiculturalism. The student's reason for feeling betrayed was that she had assumed I believed the same as the far-right positions of conservative Christians, with which she aligned herself. This student had taken other courses of mine in her undergraduate and graduate programs.

My pattern of self-censoring dates back to my early childhood, around the age of eight. Early 1950s. On a vacation trip from Ashland, Kentucky, to Tacoma, Washington, we visited my grandparents. One day, during a conversation, I asked my Grandfather, who was regarded as the family patriarch, if it was possible that when God created the world, He did so using evolution. (We were a family of Baptists.) His response was a swift and emphatic *NO*. My dad was there, and he sat silently. I have no recollection of where I had heard of the principle of evolution at that age. Nevertheless, my takeaway from that moment was that there were questions that were not okay to think about, much less to ask—keep those things to myself. Keeping these kinds of thoughts to myself didn't keep me from secretly questioning and believing otherwise.

Today, I wonder if I had someone whom I respected as a role model or mentor, with whom I could've thought out loud, that my life path might have been different from the path I traveled, especially during and up through the formative adolescent and early adult years. I probably would have had less anxiety about what I believed.

When I was teaching at a conservative Christian university, where I spent twenty years I would occasionally, for dramatic effect, close the door to my class room when I was about to talk about something I suspected was against what some students had been taught before venturing out to college, like the spoken or assumed doctrinal beliefs: the evils of drinking alcohol, belief in evolution, sexual relationships outside the bonds of marriage, political attitudes, abortion and so on. The students would usually snicker or roll their eyes at my theatrics of closing the door, and some probably saw me as being irreverent. As a result of this assumed lack of respect for tradition, it was not uncommon for students to request discussions about these and other topics in my office.

Although there were downsides to keeping some of my beliefs private, I was well-practiced at anticipating and addressing potential issues. The problem with total privacy is that we don't have the benefit of speaking out loud about things that we might not have realized we held strong feelings about. This is the benefit of some of the endless conversations that teenagers have with their friends. It helps to clarify one's thinking. *I didn't realize I thought that strongly about something until I said it. Or, now that I've said it, I'm not sure if that is the case.*

For growth and maturity of our thinking to take place, we need to be brave enough to look beyond what we may have accepted as being the iron-clad truth.

Foundational Assumptions of This Book

It doesn't matter which paths we may have followed, or are following, to understand the wisdom of Jesus and Buddha. What matters is that we get there. Old Testament prophets and the Buddha pointed us to the path of Jesus' wisdom, like the signs of an on-ramp to a highway. Conversely, Jesus reflects on those who had gone before him like a clarifying rear-view mirror.

Voices of contemporary psychology also reflect, or parallel, these age-old wisdoms. This is despite some psychologists' attempts to minimize or discredit the importance of religion in individuals' lives. Freud and some of his contemporaries saw religion as a crutch and an impediment to mature mental health. On the other hand, it is interesting to note that some iconic psychologists, like Carl Rogers[1], were raised in devout conservative religious families. William James, considered the father of modern psychology, wrote a landmark work on what takes place psychologically during a spiritual conversion. Carl Jung was the son of a protestant clergyman. It is said that he intended to become a minister early in his life.

It is not a stretch to realize that religious foundations have helped shape the contributions of these and other theorists to psychology, even reflecting the wisdom of Jesus and the Buddha. So, understanding that these and other wisdoms reflect one another, sometimes at a foundational level, broadens the sources of wisdom. When we automatically discount a specific source of wisdom, we may be throwing the proverbial baby out with the bathwater. Of course, this requires us to think critically about what we are hearing and reading, rather than simply believing or disbelieving something because we see it in print, listen to

---

1. Both of Carl Rogers's parents were devout Christians and raised their children attending a Pentecostal church.

it from someone we look up to, or have been told not to trust. Opening ourselves to diverse sources of wisdom enables us to gain new perspectives on older beliefs, deepening our understanding. So here's the good news: no matter where we get on the path, or which path we are on to climb the mountain, we can have confidence that we will get to the top.[2]

---

2. Matthew 7:7-8 "ask and it will be given to you; seek and you will find; knock and the door will be opened to you".

Part I

Introduction

There is a beauty in trusting that we will find God on whatever path we are searching. God does not play hide-and-seek with us by setting up a game where, if we don't happen to get the correct code or password, or if we were born and raised in a different culture, we are just out of luck. ***Seek, and you will find; knock, and the door will be open to you.*** So if we don't have the resources to make our way on one path, it's wise to search out the path you're on, or another path using the tools for that one. God will be found. Due to various circumstances, some may have become exhausted by the process and need a new perspective, even new scenery. And to our surprise, we find beauty in what others told us was a barren desert. We see a desert with streams full of life-giving water, which we require not just to survive, but to thrive.

We may have become worn out trying to find or follow God using the tools we were given in our youth: going to the church that we were taught was the only way to God, speaking the language we were taught was the only correct language for Christians, etc. Even though we may be exhausted with our old cultural ways, in our hearts and souls, we still desire to know

God; we can know him. So if I'm drawn to principles of God, kindnesses of God through psychology, or Buddhism or Native American traditions, I will still find him, provided the seeking is active and not just an idle wish.

I was raised a conservative Southern Baptist. Clear lines were drawn of who was in and who was out. Who was saved, and who was only fooling themselves. People who drank alcohol were out; tea-totalers were in. The dad of a friend of mine at church could not be a member of the church because he drove a beer truck. People who went to dances or played cards were out; abstainers were in. This gradually came to make less and less sense to me. With hindsight, I realize that as a teenager in high school, I envied the kids who attended more liberal and accepting churches, some of which even sponsored dances. Believing that if I were Lutheran, or Episcopal, or Catholic, I could go to dances on Saturday and sing in the choir on Sunday morning with a clear conscience.

Given what I've learned and have come to believe, Gay people are not automatically ruled out any more than people who drink wine and play cards are. Skin color should not be a deciding factor in who the pastor is or who can sit next to me in the pew. In the course of my adult life, psychology has come to be a core filter I use for judging wisdom and who I am. Buddhism's beliefs, which parallel sound psychology, have become the path that has led me to spiritual maturity and to believe in God again. Dietrich Bonhoeffer once said that, speaking of the Catholic Church, the church of his time had become, over the years, so great in its cultural influence that it had become an obstruction blocking the path to God. He also seemed to believe the national Protestant church of Germany had evolved to the same position when it aligned itself with Hitler and the Third Reich. This, of course, led him to support and lead the Confessing Church, which stood in opposition to Hitler and the Third Reich.

Two examples from my family come to mind of victims of obstructions erected by churches that exhibited powerful cultural influence and, as such, blocked the paths that those churches could have been helpful guides to God. The first was my maternal Grandmother. She committed what was seen at the time by fellow Baptists as an almost unpardonable sin. She got a divorce and then married a man in the church who had also been married before. They were both ostracized by the church, including their circle of friends, whom they had known for decades. So they lost the source of spiritual guidance and social support. And the church, in turn, lost them as well.

The second is my father-in-law, a man I have much respect for. At one point in his adult life, he was active in the conservative church he and his family attended. Even though he lacked formal education, completing only the eighth grade, he was an intellectually bright and critical thinker. He was a hard-working logger from Northwestern Canada. He was also a Native American. His large family had moved from the Great Lakes region of the U.S. when he was three. By putting two and two together, we have concluded over the last twenty years that a possible motivating factor for moving was the removal of Indian children from their families and placing them in boarding assimilation schools in the early to mid 1900s. He never talked about his Native American heritage, never. My wife and her cousins were always told they were French Canadian to account for their slightly darker complexion. Again, the assumption we have made in recent years about his family's race, that they were French Canadian, had to do with both the taking of native children into the 1960s, along with the prejudice and racism of the mid-1900s.[1] The goal of *assimilation* of the children was to

---

1. In recent years, as we have researched and attended some gatherings of Native American tribes, other people my wife's age have told us that they, too, were always told they were French Canadian to account for their slightly darker complexion.

essentially erase their Indian culture, including their native language, so that they could behave like good European Americans.

Coupling this racism and prejudice that he had been raised with, including Conservative Christian obstacles to finding God, it is easy to understand why he wanted little to do with Christian people who held themselves up as examples of Christ. Even though he talked very little about these people, the few times he did, it was clear he didn't want to be associated with the materialistic religious people who always seemed to have their hand out to raise money for their own interests, including the televangelists. They took advantage of people, were too shrewd in their business dealings, and treated people dishonestly. So he concluded that since that was the way church people behaved, he didn't want anything to do with them or that brand of Christianity. He didn't want to be called Christian. Yet, he lived his own personal life as a Christian. He cared for people and respected others regardless of their skin color. He freely gave of himself, even when he didn't have it to spare. This man was Christian, even though he hadn't had good examples to lead him. He concluded that the cultural lifestyle, which was called Christian, he wanted no part of. But in fact, he lived a Christian life more than many of the Christians around him.

These two examples may seem irrelevant to some, or even "get over it" to others. Granted, many people have overcome obstacles to their faith, setting aside encumbrances, as the writer of Hebrews states in the New Testament. However, due to our humanity, not everyone is capable of setting aside ingrained hurdles from early childhood or even early adulthood. For some, being raised in rigid and enmeshed environments is akin to brainwashing that sets the limits on what they can think critically about. What is often needed is a paradigm shift, a 180-degree change in how they view their world at large, or at least how they understand their own spirituality.

In this book, I explore and suggest some different paths to God. These may be paths that have heretofore been considered unthinkable, or even heretical. As I used to tell my students, there is no need to be afraid of thinking critically about the essential things of life. This is especially true if we really trust the Spirit of God in us to be with us as we seek.

Since wisdom is wisdom wherever we find it, I present three sources of wisdom that overlap, parallel, and reinforce each other. This by no means is an exhaustive treatise on wisdom. I explore psychology as one source of wisdom. I've worked and studied the field of psychology for over 50 years. I also explore Christianity as another source of wisdom. I was born into and raised as a Christian. I just turned 80. I began developing an appreciation for Buddhism and see it as an invaluable source of wisdom since my time in the late 1969s in the Vietnam War. I began a more in-depth study of Buddhism 25 years ago.

Chapter One

Back Stories

Psychologies

To best understand a person, teacher, parent, or writer, it helps to understand what influenced their development—their *back story*. Theories in psychological science are continuously developed in response to contemporary society and often built on previous theories and beliefs. Many of Freud's theories were developed in response to earlier beliefs that human beings are born with invariable innate characteristics that determine the course of their lives. Thus, royalty gave birth to the next generation of royalty, including kings and queens. Likewise, children born to peasants were doomed to be peasants—they were born that way. So Freud developed his perspectives on human behavior and development in reaction against this commonly held perspective. He developed theories of identity development, which posited that the first five years of a person's life significantly shape their future development. People *develop* into who they are. They weren't just born that way. Since this was during the Victorian era of sexual suppression and guilt, many of his patients had hangups about their sexuality. These hangups were, he came to believe, the cause of anxiety, depression, psychoses, and so on. This led him to believe that a person's basic identity was rooted in psycho-sexual urges that had been suppressed. He believed that psychoanalysis was the tool of choice to correct, or at least cope adequately with, the damage of the first five years.

Other psychological theorists came along and either expanded or deviated dramatically from Freud's psycho-sexual views of early development. Erik Erikson, for one, stated that what was most important up through our adolescent years was the psycho-*social* environment. Saying the social environment had a significantly more substantial impact on a person's development than did the first five years of psycho-*sexual* influences. Then B.F. Skinner and other learning theorists emerged, asserting that we are essentially born as a blank slate, tabula rasa. When we are born, we essentially learn through reinforcement to behave, think, and relate. J.B. Watson's behaviorism expanded on Aristotle's and St. Ignatius Loyola's assertions that it is the environment of our early years that shapes us through learning. By controlling the environment, Watson said, he could bring up a doctor, lawyer, artist, merchant-chief, and, yes, even a beggar and a thief, regardless of their talents or inclinations. He believed that the controlled environment shaped an individual's interests and preferences.

We need to have an understanding of what has gone before to adequately comprehend the theories that explain how we arrived at our current state.

It's easy to imagine that the social environment of the day influenced each theorist's perspective. For instance, the suppression of sexuality in the Victorian era had a significant impact on Freud's views. This, in turn, spawned later thinking of those who came after him. Each revision by necessity prunes some things that we realize no longer fit, and grafts or adds new thinking.

Erikson's Stages of Psychosocial Development

Approximate Age	Psycho Social Crisis
Infant-18 months	Trust vs. Mistrust
18 months-3 years	Autonomy vs. Shame & Doubt
3-5 years	Initiative vs. Guilt
5-13 years	Industry vs. Inferiority
13-21 years	Identity vs. Role Confusion
21-40 years	Intimacy vs. Isolation
40-65 years	Generativity vs. Stagnation
65 and older	Ego Integrity vs. Despair

Developmental theories tend to be true generally, but not specifically—there are always specific exceptions to a general rule.

Provided we don't insist on throwing out the baby with the bathwater at each turn, the confluence of thinking over time deepens and broadens our understanding.

This echoes a Buddhist principle of interconnectedness and interdependence. In short, no one develops in a vacuum. Throughout our lives, we are shaped by our interactions with others. I'll talk in more detail about this later in the book.

Developmentalism

The psychological principle of Developmentalism parallels this idea. This branch of psychology permeates the field of psychology across many theoretical disciplines. Many theories utilize developmental principles. Erik Erikson's theories of Psycho-Social stages serve as a good example[1]. Parents, of course, are aware of the often-mentioned terrible twos. This is where the child learns to say *No*, which accompanies the awareness that they exist apart from their parents. This is the beginning of establishing their own identity. Erikson's stages occur in a specific order and are associated with distinct age groups. Each stage has a particular set of tasks to accomplish, which sets the stage for the next stage. 'No' behavior is visited again and again, in entirely the same manner, throughout development. The arguments that occur during the pre- and early teenage years are often stressful, mainly because the *arguing* is the critical issue, not necessarily what the teen and parent are arguing about. The ability to discuss/debate one's point of view is essential for later development, as we learn to stand for what we believe. The success of accomplishing the tasks contributes to how the subsequent stage is managed. A stage can be failed or succeed. Unlike Freud's Psycho-Sexual stages, Erikson believed it is possible to go back and work through a stage that may have been problematic the first time in that stage. Earlier mistakes and struggles do not doom us to struggle with the same issue continually. We can correct earlier learning and learn more effective ways of dealing with our world.

Other stage theories are not necessarily age-locked, but they do follow a specific order and require a set of skills to accomplish. One such theory is Maslow's *Hierarchy of Needs*, a concept associated with Humanism.[2] The belief is that this drive to Self-Actualize is part of the human spirit. Progress, or transitions, to a subsequent stage requires having accomplished a previous

---

1. Erikson, Erik H. (1968) *Identity: Youth and Crisis,* Norton & Company

2. Humanism emphasizes the inherent potential value and goodness of all human beings. Emphasis is on everyday human needs and seeking solely rational ways of solving human problems.

Maslow's Hierarchy of Needs

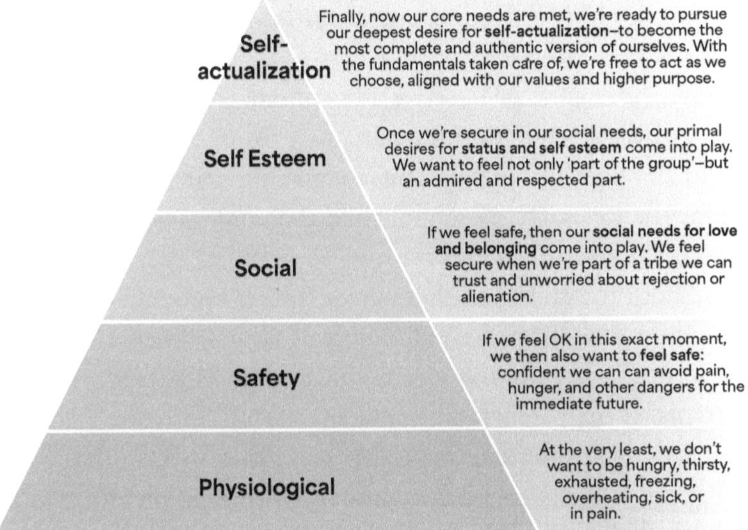

Developmental theories tend to be true generally, but not specifically—there are always specific exceptions to a general rule.

stage. Once a stage has been achieved, paradoxically, it is no longer the individual's primary focus. The stages follow a particular order: from the first stage, Psychological Needs, to the second, Safety, to the third, Social, to the fourth, Self-esteem, and to the fifth, Self-Actualization. The first three stages are seen as crucial, and if not achieved, the individual is said to be in deficit. It is similar to building a foundation before constructing the house's frame. The last stages are considered to be growth needs. If the foundational stages are not satisfied, the growth stages will not develop, or at least will be incomplete. It's said that when a person has become Self-Actualized, the final stage, they are no longer concerned with the *self* to the extent they were earlier. This is similar in some ways to Buddhism's achievement of Awakening.

A somewhat parallel concept of stage-wise development is also evident in Buddhist thought. In Buddhism, the past is considered irrelevant because one is no longer there. The present stage is new. You are always a new self. You haven't been here before. So a new perspective is required. Parents who do not recognize this and continue parenting in the same way as their child develops are in for some rough times. If they attempt to guide their elementary school child the same way they parented that child when the child was two years old, they will only frustrate both the child and themselves. This is especially true when the child transitions into adolescence. The primary task of adolescence is establishing a sense of identity separate from one's parents. If the parents of a fourteen-year-old insist on rules and restrictions appropriate for eight- or nine-year-olds, the son or daughter is likely to rebel against those rules in an effort to establish their independence. This is the reason that the *Just Say No* approach to drugs, alcohol, and sexual activity, which First Lady Nancy Regan promoted, was developmentally inappropriate for adolescents. Adolescents have developed cognitively to the point that they are no longer the same *individuals* they were a few years prior and are beginning to think critically about their world. Young children respond to and need straightforward, concrete rules to follow within their families. But adolescents are developing the ability to reason why something is inappropriate. Thus, the approach to parenting a teenager should facilitate and encourage decision-making while they are still living at home. Buddhism's concept of impermanence of the self comes to play here. Since a child has changed from who they were, approaches to discipline should be adjusted accordingly. No one is the same as they were last year, a few months ago, or even yesterday. There is no such thing as a fixed, permanent self.

Religions

As discussed earlier, the importance of the backstory should also be applied to the development of major religions and to doctrinal subsets of beliefs within those religions.

Provided we practice looking forward, truth always points to more truth. Buddhism emphasizes the importance of being present, rather than clinging to the past. This applies to beliefs, including recently discovered ones and new understandings. In clinging to old beliefs, we develop habitual patterns that can become entrenched doctrine and stop our continued development both psychologically and spiritually. There is a Buddhist koan, a parable, about an old man who walks very stooped over. All he sees is the ground in front of him. While he may find an occasional interesting rock or lost coin, he misses the views of the mountains around him and the birds that live in the trees.

This Buddhist koan/parable suggests that entrenched doctrines often leave us walking hunched over, looking down, and seeing only a few feet in front of us, much like an animal. We miss seeing what is on the horizon as well as what is in our peripheral vision. Thus, we miss discovering the new part of the world we are traveling in. By constantly looking down, we're only studying what we already know. These old, over-learned doctrines often become like a crutch or a cane that we hold on to desperately. This is an example where Freud's assertion that religion is like a crutch actually was correct. We believe we can't let go of the cane because we will fall over if we don't cling to it. By staying hunched over and only looking down, we may find an occasional coin or interesting rock. But these can hardly compare to the discovery of new truths and perspectives. The solution? Follow what we do know, stand up straight, but hold those beliefs loosely, not clinging for dear life. If we need to use a cane, such as yours truly, be sure the cane is tall enough and fits us so we can walk upright. We must allow all things to pass away, and for all things to become new.

There are many analogies about the perils of holding on too tightly. When I was a Corrective Therapist at the VA, part of my responsibilities included supervising an exercise clinic for inpatients. When a patient was riding a stationary exercise bike, we had to teach them not to gr the handlebars with a death grip. Holding on too tightly could raise their blood pressure. Which, of course, in the extreme, would result in a literal 'death' grip. So they needed to learn how to hold on with just enough strength to feel safe, but not too tightly.

I wrote a paper several years ago on how some people are drawn to the process of changing religions as a path of growth.[3] The paper described the process one goes through as they change from one major Christian denomination to another. I used my religious pilgrimage as a template for that paper, and for a memoir I published in 2024. My own journey also influences this writing.[4] I progressed from my Appalachian Kentucky Southern Baptist roots, through Pentecostalism in the Vietnam War while stationed in Thailand, to the Jesus People, to Anglicanism and Episcopalianism, and eventually *adding* the philosophy and psychology of Buddhism. As I progressed along this journey, I came to see it as a dynamic process. At times, this felt almost like a drive within me, accompanied by a curiosity for answers that are beyond the simplicity of what I had been taught in Sunday School and church. This curiosity has come with choices. Either to accept answers unquestioningly as a part of some unquestioning

---

3. Henning, Doug (2005) *Changing Religious Loyalties: a Seeker's Journey*, C.S. Lewis Summer Institute, OxBridge, Oxford, England. This paper was originally published in C.S. Lewis Institute Archives.

4. Henning, Douglas (2024). *From there to Here: Many threads of deconstruction*, SacraSage Publishing

faith, which would be denying that the questions were there in the first place. Or to explore the new horizons and possibilities for what it has to offer. The cost of temporary denial is a frustration with the status quo and even a sense of hypocrisy in appearing to go along to get along. At the same time, I've always resisted the temptation to throw the baby out with the bathwater, because usually some of what I believed seemed faithful and wise.

Hearing the same doctrine presented in the same way year after year can result in boredom and a loss of interest—the dynamism is missing. The risk here is that one's faith becomes only a lifestyle, or no different than a social club. Tuning it out and ceasing to grow leads to stagnation and the belief that one's faith has nothing new to offer. Churches are facing dwindling memberships and the loss of older members, often because their primary focus is on building a Sunday School for children. When churches attempt to attract parents but fail to develop ministries for middle-aged and older adults, they are likely to lose those individuals who could serve as mentors and vital guides through their later years. Losing the middle-agers really is tragic. Middle-agers, having developed beyond their young adulthood, could serve as critical mentors to those coming behind them.

Repeating the same teachings can lead to a failure to attract adults who do not have children or are primarily focused on career, social issues, and social justice. Several Christian denominations are presently faced with a new younger adult population, such as LGBTQ+. When the presentation of the gospel discriminates against this population, the church loses the opportunity to learn from this community of believers, as well as straight people who are supportive of this dynamic population. In Buddhist vernacular, these denominations cling so tightly to the past that the present and future pass them by. The five words of a dying church: *we've never done that before.* The clinging and grasping to past doctrines always causes the pain of a stagnant ministry. This is a failure to focus on the *Now*. The only thing we have is the present.

A lifestyle of progressing through various religious denominations, as I have, isn't without its sacrifices and challenges. Friends that we gain often don't understand our progression and can't stay friends when we move on. Additionally, in the process of understanding our own motivations for change, we can focus too much on the negative aspects that motivated us to leave the old version of faith, and forget that there were indeed positive aspects to that old community as well. We generalize what we found problematic to the entire faith or to all its people. An example of this happened just recently. We attended a memorial service for a longtime friend and saw old friends we had not seen in thirty-five years or more. It was great to see all these people with whom we had a history. My initial reason for changing from that old religious group was its lack of concern and ministry to people on the margins: people of color, LGBTQA+ individuals, people with low or no incomes, and people experiencing homelessness. Over the years, I had subconsciously developed the assumption that none of those old friends would have seen the social world the way I do today. While catching up with these lifelong friends. Some of my assumptions confirmed by *some* of the people who have gotten sidetracked into Christian Nationalism and white supremacist thinking: people of color are less than; we have no responsibility to our neighbors, and refugees are not our responsibility. They should be rounded up and shipped home. The fact that they are in need is their own problem. Power and political influence are more important than feeding the poor.

However, I was happy to see that my prejudices were, at least in some cases, incorrect. The person the service was for was a pastor and former colleague, as well as an academic, with whom

I had worked. Many of the people who spoke in his memory discussed the ministry he had developed, which served the homeless in his city. We sat behind a couple of gentlemen who, by their dress, were poor and possibly homeless. As time went on, and as I've reflected on that evening, my respect for this friend grew significantly. I was glad to see that some of these people are good individuals who share my concerns.

I've moved away from the doctrine of conservative Christianity and Evangelicalism. A lot of the practices in the name of Christianity today are misguided, to say the least, such as the nationalism and weaponization of the religious right. These perspectives and behaviors are a direct hindrance to understanding Jesus' teachings and to living out the gospel of Christ. Yet, I was humbled by the reminder that, as individuals, these are essentially good people and that not all conservative Christians are like the picture that is often portrayed by the media. I realize that there are theologically conservative evangelicals who are deeply religious, spiritual, and progressive. They're working for the rights of LGBTQA+ people, people experiencing homelessness, are doing crucial social justice work, and are working to protect and care for immigrants who are seeking a better life by coming to the United States.

I've found that through the application of Buddhist principles, practices, and spirituality, when combined with my more Progressive Christianity and sound psychological practice, it fits the world as it exists. This is not one *OR* the other, but a combination of all three simultaneously. Similar to the confluence of three rivers, which come together to form one larger and more encompassing body of water.

Chapter Two

Developmental Models of Faith

Although change is often stressful, this kind of stress can be a sign of growth, much like the growing pains that accompany physical development. Developmentalism can provide a sense of direction and assurance that better things are ahead. Several models have been proposed over the last several decades. I'll describe two models of spiritual and psychological development that I have found helpful. They apply to individual development and can be readily applied to organizations such as churches and larger religious denominations.

Kurt Lewin

First, I'll describe one scenario that can help with planned change. Kurt Lewin, a German-American psychologist, developed theories of social psychology that enhanced our understanding of how organizations change. Healthy organizations consist of a mix of *locals* and *cosmopolitans*. Locals are part of the social community that has invested itself in the social fabric and provides stability. They tend to own property and have jobs that they've had for an extended period of time. They understand how the organization reached its current state. As such, they have experienced its history and have a lot to lose if change occurs haphazardly or recklessly. Cosmopolitans, on the other hand, are invested primarily in what exists today. They tend to be energetic and often bring a sense of vision and a focus on the future. They are the renters who don't have as much to lose and usually think outside the box. Healthy social organizations need a blend of both. Each type respects the other's point of view. Locals exercise healthy caution against moving too quickly, while cosmopolitans keep the organization up to date on current trends.

Although planned change primarily applies to organizations, it also has relevance for individuals. If we become too attached to our past and avoid change at all costs, we will stagnate and fail to grow. In Buddhist parlance, this refers to clinging to the past and holding onto it too tightly. Whether that past is positive or negative. Clinging is a natural part of life, and yet it is the source of pain. Allowing the past to be the past, and being present in the Present Moment, is the secret to a healthy life.

Nothing ever stays as it is. We are always in the process of becoming, or arriving. Even the *Self* is transient. Never being the same as it was in the past, and will be different in the future from who it is today, it can be said that a stable form of self doesn't exist. A sense of constant transformation is who we are. While this is easier to see in the larger transformations that take place in our lives, gradual transformations and more subtle changes in direction can be just as impactful. This is true for spiritual conversion. Some transformations are radical and sudden, a 180-degree shift in direction. Other transformations can be less radical and take place over time. Step-wise transformations are a helpful way to view this process. It begins with an initial transition. This first step is facilitated by an attempt to answer some troubling life questions. The second step involves coming to grips with particular claims of a faith system. The third step consists of an immersion that extends beyond a casual understanding to the depths of a transformed life. The fourth stage is consistent with a total transformation. A Buddhist would say that this conversion is ongoing throughout our lives; the total transformation results in a shift in the formation of a new habitual center of personal energy[1].

Psychological benefits accompany the transformative nature of a spiritual experience. It can provide a sense of meaning in one's life, as well as comfort in knowing that we are part of something larger than just our individual existence. The transformational conversion is not complete until all four steps are accomplished. A pastor friend and mentor of the Anglican tradition used to say that getting saved happened instantly. But conversion takes a lifetime.

Conversion is typically viewed as a complete departure from one thing and the adoption of something entirely new. However, in the context of this book, the same process applies to adding something new to an existing system. In 1980, during my doctoral studies at Oregon State University, it was not uncommon for members of the church we attended to infer that I must have been a psychology student before I became a Christian. The implication was that they felt bad for me that now that I was a Christian, everything I had invested in my psychology education would be of no use—that the two philosophies could not co-exist. Occasionally, I would explain how my Christian faith and belief in psychology were quite compatible. Most of the time, I'd smile and thank them for their concern, or deflect

---

1. James, William (1902) *Varieties of Religious Experience*, Random House of Canada, Toronto

the conversation to something less heavy. Like how the OSU basketball team was doing this season, or the weather. (During the early '80s, OSU did very well on the basketball court.)

The conversion from being either a Christian or a psychologist, one or the other, to being both a Christian and a psychologist followed a path similar to that described above. I don't recall being conflicted about these two aspects of myself. I've found the same to be true in adding Buddhism to my psychology and Christianity. This all seems like a logical progression. I can recall a specific period when I felt that I had fully immersed myself in the study of Buddhism. Similarly, in the study of psychology, and earlier in Christianity.

James Fowler

James Fowler presents a second model of Spiritual Development.[2] *Primal* and *Intuitive-Projective Faith* make up the first two stages. Being dependent is the hallmark of these first stages. Dependable people go away, but are trusted to come back. As we progress toward stages four and five, the faith gradually becomes more or less conscious. A sense of self develops through the mother's reflection as we learn to talk about and create a sense of right and wrong. Similarly, we learn to speak and think in faith terms through our relationship with others. Because at this point in our cognitive development, we view our world primarily in black-and-white terms, fear is often learned here, accompanied by the belief that a devil is out to get me if I'm bad. Since our world is made up of ourselves and our immediate family, we develop the idea that we are the center of the universe. If

---

2. .Fowler, James, W. (2000) *Becoming Adult, Becoming Christian: Adult Development & Christian Faith,* Jossey Bass Publishers, San Francisco

Fowler's Stages of Faith Development

Stage 6	Universalizing Faith *Transforming process*
Stage 5	Conjunctive Faith *Awareness of perspective*
Stage 4	Individual/Reflective Faith *Focus upon personal faith*
Stage 3	Synthetic/Conventional Faith *Commitment to church & leaders*
Stage 2	Mythic/Literal Faith: Childhood *Limited to concrete thinking*
Stage 1	Intuitive/Projective Faith: Early Childhood *Images & stories*

**Developmental theories tend to be true generally, but not specifically—there are always specific exceptions to a general rule.*

something good happens, it is because I've been good. If something bad happens, it's my fault because we've been bad.

The third stage begins about the time a child starts school. This *Mythic-Literal Faith* is characterized by concrete, literal thinking and is associated with stable concepts such as time, space, and causality. Thus, there is less dependence on feeling and fantasy. The world is more predictable and orderly. Right and wrong, good and evil, accompany a sense of fairness and reciprocity. This is the time when concrete thinking incorporates the concept that good behavior is rewarded and bad behavior is punished. As such, knowing the rules becomes essential, and we are known by the groups to which we belong, such as the Baptists, Republicans, athletic teams, choir members, and so on.

Both adolescents and adults can occupy this stage. Some adults may remain in this stage throughout their lives.

Stage four is a stage of transition, *Synthetic-Conventional.* Everything that was known absolutely becomes provisional. Even though this can be an unsettling time, it is also a time of exploration and discovery of a much broader world of all things, including faith. This can feel like a time of crisis for both the individual and those closest to them. It's a time of questioning. It's a time of reworking, if not all things, at least some of the essential things. This is the transition from Concrete thinking, characterized by absolute knowing, to Formal thinking, which enables thinking in the "what if" mode. Because this is the pre-teen to early adolescence age, the '*just say no*' approach to decision making about drugs and alcohol is developmentally inappropriate. An absolute "No" may be appropriate for younger children under the heading of family rules. But not for adolescents. They need guidance on critical thinking. Because transitions are never a smooth straight line, teenagers may appear unstable: mature as a twenty-five-year-old earlier in the day, and childish later in the same evening, arguing over Legos. The sense of *self* is also vulnerable. The typical younger adolescent can change their minds about things several times in one day. As they move into later adolescence, this up-and-down thinking tends to even out into a more steady stream of thought.

Synthesis of belief and values is taking place. Thus, the faith they are developing, which begins with identifying with a group of peers, is progressing to more individual ownership. This is the prelude to examining the previously unexamined values and beliefs. The challenge for parents and those working with youth groups is to allow this upcoming period of examination to unfold in a supportive and reflective manner. This is the beginning of wisdom, which comes in starts and spurts. The use of acquired knowledge, life experience, understanding, and insight to make judgments becomes evident. Saying that certain things should not be questioned or spoken aloud does not work and is apt to alienate the individual. For individuals who convert to a faith system as adults, the process is the same, except that the time spent in each stage is usually compressed.

Stage five of faith development: Individuative-Reflective Faith. *Self*-authorization is being developed. *Other self*-authorization is being extinguished. This is a time of critical choosing of beliefs, values, and commitments, of examining previously held doctrines and beliefs. When this process is delayed into later years, or denied altogether, it can take on crisis proportions, even a midlife crisis. Father Richard Rohr offers a helpful metaphor.[3] In the first half of life, in Western cultures, we are busy building the exterior aspects of our lives: obtaining an education, finding a spouse, having children, and establishing a career. The things that people see. The second half of life is building the interior of who we are. Developing and being accountable for ourselves, and allowing the chaff we've collected and clung to as we built the exterior to blow away. This chaff we have brought along as excess baggage is the cause of the pain we all experience.

The second and third of the *Four Truths of Buddhist thinking* are that this pain, being the *result of clinging* desperately to what we've accumulated, *can be alleviated*. By ceasing to cling and grasp, the pain also ceases to exist. The Beatles' song, *Let It Be*, comes to mind here, . . . *when I find myself in times of trouble*, . . . *words of wisdom, let it be*—**let it go.**

Stage six, Conjunctive Faith, is most common in midlife, at thirty-five, and beyond. This is the conjunction of opposites. Fowler describes this as an ". . . integration of elements in our-selves, in society, and our experience of ultimate reality [which]

---

3. Rohr, Richard, (2011), *Falling Upward: A Spirituality for the Second Half of Life,* Jossey Bass.

have the character of being apparent contradictions, polarities, or paradoxical elements".[4] If growth is to continue, the more rigid boundaries of the social groups to which we belong begin to soften and become more permeable. The swagger of the confident ego from the previous stage begins to give way to more humility.

Additionally, there is a coming to grips with the fact that some, if not many, of our behaviors and thought patterns are, to a large extent, not unchangeable. We do change and grow through our lives. This is who we are. This is where we find mindfulness meditation helpful. In Buddhist meditation, we find peace by letting go of past failures and successes, which, because they are in the past, we cannot change. Nor are we preoccupied with paralyzing worries of the future, over which we have little control anyway. Further, mindfulness meditation allows us to let go of, or at least loosen our grip on, the concerns and things we are preoccupied with daily.

Conjunctive Faith is marked by the realization that all things must be made new, while faced with being deeply invested in the present order of things. This can present a genuine conundrum, or even a crisis of faith, as we come to desire transformation into newness.

The Universalizing Faith is the seventh stage of faith development. The transition into a transformation with the ". . . ultimate conditions of life."[5] In many ways, this is what Buddhism calls the Ultimate Truth. This Ultimate Truth is often beyond the words that we understand when trying to describe our new insights. Conventional Truth, on the other hand, is what we experienced as our fabrication of what we saw in the present.

---

4. Fowler, James, W. (2000) *Becoming Adult, Becoming Christian: Adult Development and Christian Faith,* Jossey Bass, pg 51.

5. ibid, pg 55.

These fabrications, although meaningful, are entirely culturally and time-specific. Therefore, conventional truth is specific to the time in which we live. As such, conventional truth will change over time. The ultimate truth stretches across time. Conventional truth, as influenced by the Ultimate Truth, results in *qualitative and broadened perspectives*—these are the paradigm shifts that produce newness. According to Fowler, those Universalizing Faith individuals "*. . . seem to have undergone an experience of the negation of ties and affections that we* [have] *generally taken to be 'natural'.*[6] They felt natural because they occurred gradually at a subconscious level.

The reason for emphasizing the practicality of stage development is to point out how, by the very nature of living, we are always in a new place. Yesterday and this morning are gone. This afternoon is new to me. So, in letting the past go away and welcoming the present, I'm always starting over. No scorekeeping. The past, even a few moments ago, is irrelevant, and the future is never here. I'll talk more about this later in sections on Buddhism. Buddhism and Mindfulness meditation bring excellent and necessary tools for staying in the moment, in the *Now.*

The writers of the Old Testament predicted and influenced the religious beliefs of Jesus' time as well as the beliefs he came to espouse. Some of his teachings supported those earlier teachings, while others did not. For example, he said that "it's written that you should not commit murder, or take another man's wife. But Jesus expanded this to saying, even if you *think* about killing or about adultery in your heart, dwelling on this in your thoughts, you are as guilty as if you had done it. He seemed to want everyone to realize that none of us is perfect and all need redemption, a new birth. Further, that even in our imperfections, we are who we are and worthy of being loved. From this, it is logical to

---

6. Ibid. pg 59

assume that being an imperfect human may not be that big of a deal. It depends on what we do with these imperfections.

It should be evident that Old Testament writers, teachers, and spiritual leaders were influenced by the contextual cultural influences of their time, as seen in the works of Jeremiah, King David, Ezra, and Nehemiah. An additional cultural influence in Egypt around 400 BCE was the spread of Hinduism and Buddhism.

I always told my students when they were embarking on a writing assignment that they should never be satisfied with just what a new writer has to say in their most recent iteration of older, established theories. Always look for backstories. How did they arrive at their current position? Who influenced the current theorists? What was going on culturally and socially? Go to a source to help set the context of what newer writers are saying. Understanding the backstory actually gives the current truth or version even more power.

Psychology

As an example, Albert Ellis and Arron Beck developed their ideas of Cognitive Behavior in response, in part, to B.F. Skinner's and J.B. Watson's behaviorism. Beck and Ellis held that cognitive behavior is similar to physical behavior in that much of our mental life is learned through and reinforced by the same mechanisms, such as reinforcement: operant and classical conditioning. Not so much from innate drives as psychoanalytic theorists believe. As such, our thoughts, which get paired with cues from our environment, are amenable to change just like other behaviors. So Cognitive Behavior theory believes that it's our thought patterns that are the source of psychological problems such as depression, anxiety, and obsessive-compulsive disorders. Granted, we are born with genetic tendencies toward these, but our thought patterns reinforce and strengthen them. Of course, as with all subsequent theoretical innovations, things are rarely as simple as that. For example, the treatment of choice can be more sophisticated, involving decisions about which counseling approach is best suited for a specific individual and whether medical or medication treatment should also be part of the process.

The parallel premise of Developmental Psychology states that we are constantly changing as we go through various stages in our lives. As children, our perspective changes from the way we see things at four years old to how we view the world as we progress through elementary school, middle school, high school, and into adulthood. Further, each stage sets the stage for the next stage. We see the world, in part, based on how we viewed things in the previous stage. Depending on how realistic or unrealistic those views were in the last stage, we will carry that realism or unrealism over as a foundation for the following stage(s). If we cling too tightly to a previous stage, to the childish beliefs of six- and seven-year-olds, through adolescence, we find ourselves frustrated with the world of young adulthood and beyond. Clinging and grasping are, in the beliefs of Buddhism, what cause pain in our lives. This is why late adolescents and young adults often find the religion in which they were raised impractical. If they think this is all there is, they look elsewhere for foundational beliefs, such as education, politics, and so on. This is also what the frequent arguments between parents and teenagers are about. The teenager is challenging what they find as unfair, unreasonable, or impractical. They are in the process of sorting out what will be important to them as they mature. At times, the force with which the adolescent voices their objections may seem extreme, given the context of the debate. This is because they are in the early learning stages of figuring out how strongly they believe something and how to express it. I heard it said several years ago that living with teenagers is like getting slowly pecked to death by a flock of geese.

When I was doing couples therapy, it was not uncommon for one or both of them to comment that the other had changed from who they were when they were younger. Even though I didn't always say so out loud, my initial thought was, well, no kidding, I hope this forty-year-old person with three kids sitting in my office isn't still acting and thinking as they did at twenty-five.

Change, even when it's needed and wanted, can be stressful. When people are in the midst of significant change or stress in their lives, they sometimes try to revert, at least for a while, to behaviors that provided security or comfort in the past. The attraction of these old patterns is that they are well learned habits. This regression seldom works for very long. When regressions last for extended periods, such as a few years or more, they can cause personal chaos or even a crisis.

Midlife transitions are a predictable phase of life marked by significant changes. As we move from younger adulthood to midlife, this time occasionally develops into a midlife crisis of varying degrees. Especially when issues from earlier in life have been overlooked or ignored. The stereotype of a forty-eight-year-old male amid a midlife crisis is having an affair with, or dating a younger woman, or even leaving his wife, getting a red sports car, tanning, and getting in shape. All the things he did at twenty, or wanted to do, which gave him a certain status in his own eyes. This form of grasping at the imagined past, within Buddhism, is what causes suffering. We're constantly changing, even if we resist it. The secret to satisfaction is accepting and embracing those changes. Each new version of who we are is here. Rejecting this fact can be a tremendous source of psychological and emotional pain and discomfort.

Life tends to go off course for everyone at times. Even predictable phases like aging, illness, loss of loved ones through death or divorce, cause what Buddhists call Dukkha—pain.

During these times of change and stress, we are often more vulnerable and susceptible to illness. There is a whole list of somatic diseases in which stress sometimes plays a part: headaches, backache, flare-ups with asthma, gastrointestinal disorders, high blood pressure, and so on. Trying to resist change or to return to the way things were, *clinging* to the present or the past, is in itself a source of pain. Meditation can be a significant help in accepting the present as it is. This kind of acceptance doesn't mean you're agreeing with or wanting what's happening. However, you take what is happening as reality. By this type of acceptance, you are removing the struggle to change what is and can deal more effectively with the present normal.

The Self

A central belief of Buddhism is that the *Self,* as a stable and predictable entity, does not exist. The concept of self comprises *five aggregates* that constantly interact with one another: consciousness, physical form, feelings, perception, and volition. Due to the constant interaction among these five aggregates, the self is constantly in flux.

Our bodies begin aging from the moment of birth. The infant has just spent nine months growing and developing. So at birth, they continue the process. We are different physically as adults from what we were as children. During the first two years of life, our brains fine-tune themselves. The brain is sculpting itself. This fine-tuning continues through adolescence and into early adulthood. We are different from what we will be as young adults, and later as middle-aged adults, and still later as older adults. Feelings, perceptions, motivations, and consciousness change through life—from day to day, moment to moment. As each aggregate changes, the aggregates adapt to accommodate that change. Mental health and spiritual maturity depend on our ability to adapt and accept these changes. Conversely, one cause of mental ill-health or suffering is the result of trying to cling to what was.

This is a principle Buddha taught and is a characteristic of all human beings. In Jesus' wisdom, he talked to Nicodemus in the New Testament about the process of new birth, being born again, which is necessary for all of us. We are constantly being born anew. It's the constant need to let all things pass away and become new. A new self is continually emerging. Jesus was referring to a principle taught by the Buddha some 400 years earlier. And in doing so, Jesus added a deeper spiritual dimension to the Buddha's psychological and philosophical teachings. That Jesus was influenced by the cultural mores of his day is obvious and evident in the parables he used to illustrate the kingdom of God. Since Buddha had also taught in that part of the world, it is conceivable, even reasonable, that Buddhism influenced Jesus. This would account for the many similarities between Buddhism and Christianity.

Chapter Three

Integrative Wisdom ——————————

Thinking Confluently

The possibility that Jesus was influenced by Buddhist culture is distinct. Jesus lived in Egypt as a child for anywhere between three and seven years or more. Buddhism had a presence in Egypt as early as 250 BCE. I will continue to connect threads from the wisdom of Buddha to the wisdom of Christ throughout this writing. I'm proposing not only a connection, but a confluence—an integration—of the two wisdoms throughout this book. This confluence is often expressed through the 150-year-old science of modern psychology.

The reason for taking this position is at least threefold. First, it lends validity to my experiences and observations over the last fifty-plus years, as well as what I've seen in others during my practice of psychology, particularly over the past 20 years as I've delved more deeply into Buddhism. In studying Buddhism, my faith has been strengthened. This has enabled me to integrate the roots of my Christian faith with the teachings of the Buddha and my academic and professional practice in psychology. Before this time, even though I've worked at and written about the integration of psychology and faith, my spirituality has at times felt somewhat compartmentalized or separate from other parts of who I am. Second, the Psychology I've studied and practiced since the 1970s fits consistently with these spiritual views.

An example is the book of Philippians in the New Testament, as well as Buddhism, which incorporates Cognitive Behavior, Existentialism, Gestalt, and Developmentalism. It is part of our human nature to want things to make sense. To connect the dots, so to speak. If you see a series of dots and dashes arranged in the shape of a letter, such as an A, you naturally recognize it as a letter rather than as a series of unconnected dots and dashes with no meaning. This is completing the Gestalt. Gestalt is, by definition, an organized whole, which is seen as more than a mere sum of its parts.

Third, I believe I'm not alone in the various struggles we face as we complete our pilgrimage. I've arrived, and I'm coming to a more integrated understanding of who I am. I hope that those who have struggled with the limits of the Christian Faith as it is presented today in Western society will find more comfort in looking beyond traditional teachings of Greek-filtered Christian thought. Thus, we can expect to see Jesus through the eyes of the Buddha. Buddha points to Jesus. Jesus' wisdom puts specific behaviors and ways of interacting with other humans into Buddha's psychology and philosophy.

The Greeks hijacked Jesus' wisdom by making it primarily a cognitive, thinking religion, rather than what should have been a healthy mixture of Eastern mysticism as well as Greek intellectualism. As Western culture Christians, we have missed out on the theoretical and philosophical understanding of the mystic awareness of language that original Buddhism had to offer Christ. Interestingly, the region where Jesus lived was the *Middle* East. Not the Far East, not the West.

Discovering the magic/mystical, *Drala,* comes through seeing things not with the eyes, but with the heart.[1] Seeing things as they are ultimately is often beyond our ability to put into words. In Buddhist thought, this is unconditioned wisdom, inherently connected to our being. This requires being open to seeing and understanding things beyond the limits of our conditioned learning. In present-day parlance, this is similar to expanding our paradigms and being open to continual paradigm shifts. *When we see things as they are, they* often *make* more *sense to us.*[2] Letting preconceived frames of reference drop away. Words do tend to get in the way, especially in the way of experiencing the mystical. Often, as soon as we put words and absolute definitions to things, we're in danger of deeper meanings slipping through our fingers. Just as we think we've finally got it figured out, it's easy to lose it.

In my world of psychology and counseling, this unconditioned wisdom is akin to believing that the solutions to life's puzzles already exist within each of us. Carl Jung developed a similar concept, that of the *collective unconscious,* which refers to a universal, inherited layer of the human psyche that contains archetypes and is shared by all individuals.

In psychology, we often discuss clinical intuition, or the trust in one's instincts. Therapy and counseling are processes of discovering what already exists within the person and helping them open their eyes to their own potential. This is the *Art* of psychotherapy. Buddhism stresses that this is the inherent good within all of humankind. Over recent years, I've heard more and more prominent Christian theologians discussing a doctrine of

---

1. Drala: the spiritual energy in the natural world found through our senses, and connecting our being with the power of the environment. . . . seeing the sacredness and wonder in the everyday.

2. Trungpa, Chogyam, (1984) *Shambhala: The Sacred Path of the Warrior,* Shambhala Publications, Inc. Boulder, CO, pg 70

original goodness rather than a doctrine of original sin. If God is indeed responsible for creation, and *God is Good,* then we cannot have been born in sin. Of course, for a lot of the old-line denominations, this sounds like heresy. But not to me. For Christians, this means seeking God in no particular way, but being aware of Him, expecting Him, and not being surprised when He appears around the next corner.[3] The *Original Good* theologians, *Open and Relational Theology (ORT),* as well as their followers, are most likely to welcome those people on the margins, including non-white individuals, refugees, LGBTQ+ individuals, people of other faith traditions, and those from non-faith traditions.[4] This is consistent with the belief in the inherent goodness of all creation.

This could certainly draw support from Developmental Psychology, which emphasizes the differences between various life stages in each of Buddhism's five aggregates: consciousness, physical form, volition, feelings, and perception. Gatherings of three generations at family reunions provide practical evidence of this. Grandparents recall how they thought and acted similarly to their grandchildren, which seems like not that long ago. Yet there are only similarities in: volition, physical appearance and abilities, speed of cognitive processing, and so forth. Buddhist teachings concerning 'self' deny the *eternal* existence of the self. Admittedly, some things do persist over time. But the thought of complete *annihilation* of self from one moment to the next is equally deniable. The Buddha taught that extremes such as these should be avoided.

Between eternalism and annihilationism lies a midpoint— *the middle way.* This middle way provides a construct of a causal

---

3. Chambers, Oswald, (1992) *My Utmost for His Highest: An Updated Edition I Today's Language,* January 25 reading

4. A few ORT authors: Brian McLaren, Thomas Jay Oord, Jonathan Foster.

connection of the five aggregates, which does persist. This casual connection between the aggregates forms a pattern of interactions referred to as *dependent arising*—a continual state of becoming and developing that is dependent on what is happening around us. One phase, or developmental stage, is dependent in part on the preceding stage and sets the stage for the following stage. Furthermore, each stage of an individual's life is powered by the experiences they have from one point in time to the next. What endures is the way the five aggregates are connected. According to the *middle way*, we neither exist from one point in time to the next, nor are we the same from one point to the next.

Family psychological studies support these uniquenesses. Within a family system, each individual has unique experiences of themselves, which facilitate the pattern of connections of their aggregates. A brother or sister has interactions and experiences with their sibling that are unique to their relationship, distinct from the experiences others have with them. These unique experiences, whether interactions with other humans, enlightenment, or simply growth and maturity, all contribute to one's individuality and continually evolving self. This growth, which is the result of interactions with our surroundings, is what Buddhism refers to as *Dependent Co-Arising*. This is, in part, what Proverbs 27:17 is referring to. That iron sharpens iron; interactions with others help improve one's character. We are all interconnected, not only with other humans, but also with all sentient beings and the Earth. Everything that exists is dependent on other beings.

We are constantly arising/developing, and therefore do not possess a stable, predictable self today that is the same as it was in the past or will be in the future. However, we are conditioned through mechanisms such as Natural Selection to learn and thus predict the future from our experiences. We learn to avoid taunting a rattlesnake based on our previous knowledge. We learn to stop at a red light. This self-protective conditioning becomes reflexive, second nature. The problem arises when we attempt to generalize this ability to predict into unpredictable aspects of our lives. We can't predict with certainty that the attainment of a particular level of consciousness or understanding will bring happiness or satisfaction in life, or even for longer than a few moments. Or that ridding ourselves of a source of physical pain will finally bring peace or satisfaction. The Rolling Stones' hit of the '60s declared they "... *Can't Get No Satisfaction*", no matter how hard they tried. Believing that trying harder to achieve what one craves or thirsts after guarantees happiness is what the Buddha taught is the cause of suffering. Always wanting something else is the source of human suffering.

I cringe when I hear motivational speakers and megachurch preachers on television say that if you want something bad enough, you can have it. All you have to do is want it bad enough. And if a person donates enough money, the minister will even pray for them to achieve their goal. This *prosperity gospel* evangelism frequently serves to bilk people who have bought into the *you can have it all if you want it bad enough philosophy, and* cling desperately to this as a sign of their faith. While at the same time making the charlatans wealthy beyond belief. What keeps people hooked on these scams is the belief that they must not have wanted whatever it was badly enough, or not have had enough faith in it. Thus, they need to contribute more money as a sign of their faith. Granted, these are extreme examples, but they illustrate the Buddha's teachings. It is not necessarily the thing one is craving that is the source of pain. It is the craving itself that is a source of pain and unhappiness for humans. For those who acquire even some of what they've been craving, they then grasp onto and hold tight to what they have, which in turn causes a new source of pain. The scriptures state that the *love* of money is the root of all kinds of evil. Money, by itself, is not the problem.[5]

In the 1970s and 1980s, I developed and directed a community counseling center for a large church in Tacoma, Washington. Although this church did not share the same level of positive-confession thinking as the ones I mentioned, it did attract a particular element of individuals who believed in the prosperity gospel. I had the opportunity to witness firsthand when people like Jim and Tammy Faye Baker from the PTL (Praise the Lord) television network,[6] and Televangelist Benny Hinn would come to town and hold week-long crusades at our church. I knew personally some of the people who would flock to these meetings and donate proportionately significant sums, grasping for blessings of wealth, health, and happiness. Some would buy time-share condominiums at the ministries' themed resorts. I've been in the homes of some lower-middle-class people and have seen their lifestyles. My parents were one of them. Others would flock to the crusades of Kenneth Copeland. These Ministries are frequently independent and interdenominational in structure, and as such, do not belong to a larger hierarchical organization. This translated to a lack of accountability, both fiscally and doctrinally, and otherwise. It is easy to see how vulnerable individuals get sucked into these schemes. But all humans, not just those from the lower middle class, are vulnerable to getting trapped in a cycle of craving and grasping, of always wanting more. This is part of human nature. Psychology, along with the wisdom of Christianity and Buddhism, offers a way out of this natural tendency.

---

5. 1 Timothy 6:10

6. In Yahoo News last spring (5/28/25), I saw that Jim Bakker was pleading that unless his viewers donate $1,000 each to raise $1 million, he would be on the street. This, of course, is after he was released in 1994 from 4 years in prison for bilking followers out of $158 million.

Granted, thanks again to natural selection, suffering is just part of life. Craving and grasping keep us on guard against enemies we think want to take away the things we cling to and believe will satisfy us. Further, once we have grasped something, we continue to hold it with a death grip. This keeps us in the hunt for things that we think will alleviate our ailments. If we can achieve a certain level of education, secure a promotion at work, acquire a car, or gain the approval of people we hold in high esteem, we will be happy and satisfied. However, following the attainment of that which we have thirsted for, our brains are built to ask, What have you done for me lately? Thus, we begin anew, craving the next thing we believe will satisfy us. Since it is natural to be in this state of envy, craving, and grasping, we have to address these tendencies, which cause pain and unhappiness, with purposefulness. This is where regular meditation comes in, serving as a tool for alleviating suffering and pain.

Mindfulness meditation helps us return to the present moment. It is always now. All we can truly be assured of is this moment, being fully present in the moment. We are never assured of the future. At the time of this writing, our government appears to be in chaos. Things are out of control. This makes us anxious and fearful. We don't know what the outcome will be. However, in reality, chaos and unpredictability are always present. It has always been and will always be. Where you are now and what you are is all you have. It is an illusion to believe that things are predictable, that if we get a specific individual out of office or into office, then things will automatically be better. Meditation allows us to focus on the present, the here and now. It's like the reset button. Arguably, we need to be aware of where things are headed and make plans accordingly. But our security and happiness can only be based in the now. We must hold lightly to plans which reach out into the distant future. No death grip on what we can only hope the future holds.

This is what Buddhism teaches. It is also what Jesus taught in the parable of the rich fool, who said he would tear down his barns and build larger ones to store even larger harvests of grain for security in years to come. He was a fool because he would die that night. Carl Rogers' *Person-Centered Psychology* stresses the importance of *being in the now,* even within the confines of he counseling office.

This was the appeal of itinerate teachers like Jesus and Buddha, who lived from one day to the next and with only the clothes they had with them. When my wife and I traveled in Southeast Asia a few years ago, we saw Buddhist Monks and Nuns on their morning rounds collecting daily sustenance and owning only what they had with them, as well as what followers would leave at the front of their houses for them. Within Buddhism, this ascetic lifestyle is considered honorable and is a far cry from what is often desired and admired in Western capitalist Christian society. Living above one's means with mountains of debt, unfortunately, is a common occurrence. Jesus' Sermon on the Mount runs counter to much of how Western Christianity is preached and its efforts to live out the gospel. The lifestyles of Christ and Buddha were humble and ascetic.

I once heard it said that a minister should aim to live a lifestyle that is at the median of the congregation that they are pastoring. Yet, in Western Christianity, especially among the prosperity gospel preachers I mentioned, living a lavish life is often admired, thought to be a sign of God's blessing, and one that congregants are encouraged to desire and strive for, grasp, and cling to. This difference between Western Christianity and Buddhism is part of what attracts me to Buddhism.

Psychologies

Many theories of psychology share elements with the world's religions. I will talk about four current perspectives in psychology that parallel the teachings of the Buddha and Jesus: Cognitive Behavioral Therapy, Viktor Frankl's Existentialism, Gestalt Psychology, and Carl Rogers' Person-Centered Therapy. Frankl emphasized the importance of finding meaning in life through devotion to a cause that is beyond oneself. Happiness doesn't come about as a result of chasing and then clinging to it. Happiness is a byproduct of being devoted to something outside oneself. Frankl asserted that circumstances in which we find ourselves are not what provides this sense of purpose or meaning, or the cause of unhappiness. Instead, it is our *reaction* to those circumstances.[7] In Frankl's backstory, he developed this existential perspective while in a concentration camp in Germany.

Cognitive-behavioral psychology emphasizes the role that perception plays in our sense of peace and well-being. The degree to which one blames circumstances or other people's behavior for their own suffering and emotional pain always interferes. "Taking responsibility" for our suffering paradoxically lessens the pain. Understanding that altering our perspective on our situation leads to satisfaction in the here and now. Nothing is as it seems. When Westerners look at a picture, they tend to see only the central part, the figure, and miss what is in the background. Even when we look in the mirror, what we see is not what others see when they look at us. What we see in the mirror is a reversal of what others see.

A Gestalt Psychology exercise is to think of a difficult situation, like a problem relationship, and say to yourself, "I take responsibility for it", rather than blaming it on someone or

---

7. Frankl, Viktor (2006) *Man's Search for Meaning,* Beacon Press, Boston

something else. Carl Rogers' Client-Centered theories are centered on being present in the *moment* and having self-expectations that align with reality. Craving to be something that doesn't match who we are leads to maladies such as anxiety and depression.

One of the goals of Gestalt Psychology is to be aware of ourselves as an integrated whole. This is in contrast to being fragmented and a victim of various external forces. Allowing that many things in life *just are*, rather than trying to alleviate all discomfort, is a key initial step toward achieving individual peace. This change in perspective is crucial. These four psychologies are considered the treatment of choice for maladies like anxiety, which has its origins in learned beliefs that shoulds and oughts are absolute rules, rather than preferences. *Thinking something "**must** not be a certain way" is quite different than thinking that "I would **prefer** things to be a certain way, but I don't necessarily have to have it be that way to be happy and survive".* When we believe something must be, or must not be, it prevents us from adapting to things as they are. Holding himself as an example, the Apostle Paul wrote to the Philippians that he had come to the place where he could be content in whatever situation he was in: fed, hungry, living in luxury, or in want.[8] (I have long thought that the book of Philippians could have been written with Buddhist teachings in mind.)

---

8. Philippians 4:11-13

PART II

Chapter Four

Buddha Instructs My Christian Faith

Buddha's teachings often appear more Christian than today's Conservative/Evangelical Christianity

Buddha as Salt: *Restoring the Soul*

The further we get away from the original starting point of a belief or philosophy, the more we tend to drift toward the average, or midpoint. As such, over time, we can see more similarities with other perspectives and fewer substantive differences than we saw initially. There are numerous theoretical schools of psychology, including psychoanalytic, person-centered, gestalt, behavioral, cognitive-behavioral, emotionally focused, Rational-Emotive, and Ego Psychology, to name a few. And many of these can have numerous variations within each one. If you were to place these on a timeline, you would see that many of them stood on the shoulders of the ones that came before. Very often, each iteration is an improvement on previous theories, or at least an adaptation that better fits particular situations/circumstances. Sometimes a new theory is significantly different.

When new doctoral psychologists are relatively young and newly graduated, they sometimes vigorously defend a particular theoretical orientation. Yet, research suggests that as we get older and gain more experience, many of us from differing schools of thought tend to look more similar than do new psychologists from within the same orientation. We become more *eclectic,* drawing from a range of perspectives and using what works. The result is often a better fit than just pulling a set of beliefs off the rack.

When I taught at a conservative Christian Protestant university in the Midwest, I occasionally received questions from students expressing their hesitations to consider thoughts and ideas from outside "the box" of their conservative roots. These hesitations often extended to ideas originating in other Christian doctrines, such as Catholicism, or those considered more liberal, such as Lutheranism and Episcopalianism. For example, some students became nervous at the suggestion that evolution is widely accepted as an explanation for the origin and maintenance of the world. This hesitation was especially pronounced among students whose high school was a private Christian school or who were home-schooled.

My response to their anxiety, with its roots in 1 John 4:4, was to trust that "*. . . greater is He that is in you than any external force in the world,* even the world of ideas. We don't need to be afraid of thinking critically. The advantage of viewing things from different perspectives is that it helps us see things from a slightly different vantage point. This way, we often discover characteristics we missed from viewing only one side. As I've gotten considerably older, my physique has changed dramatically, partly due to a sagging and southern drift. I gained weight following treatment for cancer a few years ago. The gained weight decided to hang around and sag, pun intended. So, when I look in the mirror, I often try to remember to look at myself head-on, rather than from the side. I've said that I have a ten-yard body. I look better from ten yards away, face on, than from a few feet and from the side.

Religious perspectives also fit into this dynamic pattern. The sharp edges that distinguish one faith from another wear down over time through interaction with other belief systems and diverse cultures. Even though I may be able to fool myself momentarily, regarding my grandpa's body, it would be foolish to believe my fabrication that I'm in the same physical condition that I was in thirty or forty years ago. I may be in good enough shape for an 80-year-old, but not compared to a fit 50-year-old.

When we take a risk to consider the inconceivable, one of two paradoxical insights can come. Either we realize that what we were afraid to consider is not that different from what we believe, or the new perspective really does enhance our understanding, and maybe I was wrong about this or that. This is called learning and growth.

When conducting couples counseling with a couple struggling in their relationship, they often feel that their differences are irreconcilable. Yet, they believe that the only option is to endure and suffer. This is usually due to religious, cultural, or social constraints. They never considered, at least out loud, separating or divorcing. Essentially, they felt stuck. Paradoxically, I would at times push them to consider how they might go about separating, including dividing up property, and how they would inform their kids and friends. Once they realized they could survive as separate individuals, if it came to that, they didn't feel as trapped in their relationship. Realizing they had a *choice* about staying together, they were freer to explore other options for resolving their differences. They could *choose* to stay or leave. This frequently set the stage for realizing that the things that they thought were so big between them might be resolvable. Or that, with acceptance, they could live with things the way they were. In addition to acceptance, tolerance, respect, and love, it requires the ability to choose, daily, to be with someone.

Generally speaking, new and broader perspectives result in adaptations and are improvements precisely because they come from different points of view. New perspectives, when we are open to them, are necessary for growth. They are paradigm shifts. In my memoir, which I wrote a couple of years ago, I described a lifelong pattern of deconstructing and examining my current spiritual, social, and psychological beliefs. The result has often been that I add some new ones and remove some older beliefs.

When we hold on to well-practiced beliefs with the tenacity of a drowning man/woman, we often sink with the inadequate fabrication of that myth. As a lifeguard in my high school days, we learned to approach a struggling swimmer from behind and let them dip just a bit lower in the water. This would cause them to relax reflexively for a brief moment. We could then grab them from behind to bring them to shore. If we approached them face-on, they might be in such a panic that they would reach for our heads, and in a self-destructive instant, push the very person under water that could save them.

In Buddhism, we learn that clinging to and grasping the mental fabrications by which we have been living is a significant source of pain and suffering. These fabrications often originate from what we've been taught as we've grown up. Or they are our original fabrication. In either case, they serve to justify our beliefs and reinforce our clinging to them.

Looking for New Perspectives

When our sons were in middle school, we often attended an Episcopal Christmas Eve service. Having been raised a conservative protestant, I found the liturgical services refreshing and enlightening. These experiences tended to make well-practiced, often rote things, seem new. To appreciate the meaning of the service and the message, we had to pay close attention to what was happening around us.

One of our early experiences of attending an Episcopal Christmas Eve Service was quite humorous. We had seen an ad in the newspaper listing the church service schedule in our city. The listing stated that the *fellowship* would be first, followed by the sermon. The fellowship would start at 10:30. Since we didn't think we would know anyone, we thought the *fellowship* portion might be a little awkward. We expected that the fellowship would be similar to what we observed at our Protestant church—coffee, punch, and cookies, with everyone milling around and chatting. However, we arrived around 10:45 p.m. and found that the service was already well underway. This would not have been a problem, except that the sanctuary was packed. That is, except for the very front row. When there was a break in between hymns, the usher escorted us down to the front. This meant that we could not observe the people in front of us to determine what actions to take, such as when to kneel, stand, or sit, or which book to use: the *Book of Common Prayer* or the *Hymnal.*

So we tried to look over our shoulders, without being too conspicuous, to see what we should be doing. We discovered that the Book of Common Prayer differed from the Book of Hymns. We also didn't know if we were allowed to partake in the Eucharist. We knew that some Protestant and Catholic churches only allowed members to participate in Communion. We realized later that, generally speaking, Episcopalians are welcoming to everyone. They encourage everyone to participate to the extent they feel comfortable.

With hindsight, I realize that I've had an almost innate drive to see things from new perspectives throughout my entire life.

This is probably one reason we enjoy traveling and visiting other cultures.

I've come to liken paradigm shifts, small and large, to adding salt and spices to food. They enhance flavor and can help preserve food. Even food that we already really like. This is what finding Buddhism has been like for me.

Much of Jesus' teaching parallels that of the Buddha. There are a few reasons that I imagine are responsible for these similarities. First, God was speaking through Buddha in the same way as he was through the Old Testament prophets. Second, Jesus was influenced by Buddhist culture and teachings. Both of these possibilities lead to the assumption that Jesus picked up where Buddha and the OT prophets left off. Or, third, the teachings of these two sage men are just different paths up the same mountain.

Chapter Five

Four Truths of Buddhism

According to Buddhism, there are four fundamental truths in life. The first truth is that all is suffering, that all joys and pleasures are fleeting and without lasting worth. The second truth is that there is a cause of our suffering. Each element of our suffering depends on what happened before. With habitual behavior, B.F. Skinner's Behaviorism, specifically Operant Behavior, states that what happens immediately before a behavior occurs serves as a cue for that behavior. This is true for both desirable and undesirable behavior. The third truth is what the Buddha experienced during his awakening: that suffering can come to an end. There can be an end to suffering. The fourth truth describes a path for life that leads to this cessation. Although suffering can be perceived as an illusion, it is actually caused by our own thinking and behavior.

A key principle of Buddhism is that the self, as a stable, unchangeable essence, does not exist. We are always in the process of change, of becoming. There are five aggregates, or elements, to our being: *consciousness, form* (our physical body), *feelings, perception, and mental formation* (volition). These constitute the

The Five Aggregates

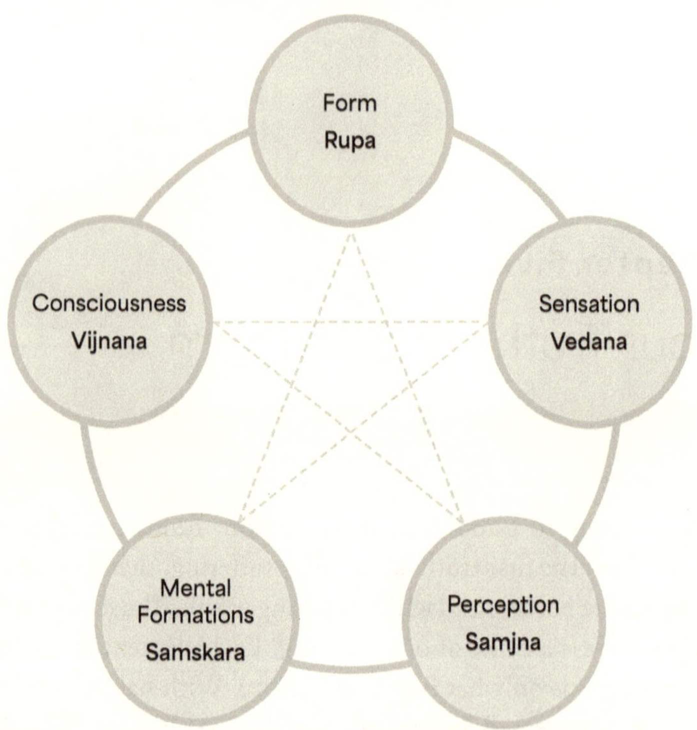

whole of a person. These five aggregates are constantly interacting with each other, and therefore, our essence is continually changing, or becoming. So we are not just one of these. We are not just our feelings, not just our perception, not just our decision(s) to use our body or mind. Our consciousness is constantly changing. When we hold on to any of these as static, the result is clinging. This clinging is needlessly false. The barrier to liberation is the clinging or grasping to one of the five aggregates. It's not so much that the self doesn't exist, but any one of these individual aggregates is not me. I'm more than this. The goal is to become estranged from these elements. We don't have to own any of these. Clinging to one or the other of these aggregates is where hatred, jealousy, and sadness come from. Therefore, they don't define me/myself.

Usually, a person is unaware of any one of these or the collective whole. Often, when we haven't thought deeply about why we act in a certain way, hold a particular opinion, or think a certain way, we create a story to fill in the blanks, so to speak, to justify our actions. We can see this when people explain why they have been lifelong members of a particular political party or a religious denomination. We feel obligated to come up with reasons why we think a specific way. But in actuality, we very often don't understand why. Then, usually, we get proficient at telling the story, and, in turn, buy into the massive fabrication that we believe defines part of who we are.

So we feed our delusions to impress others about ourselves, and we come to believe it as well. This self-promotion is very often an exaggeration of fundamental skills or traits. For example, when involved in a group project, people frequently overestimate the value and work they have contributed, possibly by as much as 140%. We see ourselves as above average. Conversely, if our project fails, we tend to attribute the cause to something outside ourselves: the teacher didn't like me, it was just bad luck, or I had the flu and wasn't feeling well. When we are successful, we often attribute our success to our abilities: I'm smart, I was well-prepared, I'm just better than the competition. When relating various experiences to others, we tend to have selective retention, remembering the positives more than the negatives. I've heard women joke that if they remembered exactly what giving birth was like, there would be more single children. These positive illusions help keep us at a task when it looks to others like we should just quit. Keeping one's head in the game is what allows us to take advantage of a positive break when—and if—it comes along.

Conversely, individuals with low self-esteem suffer from negative self-perceptions. They may not recognize a positive opportunity simply because it was unexpected. Or they may even drop out and not be around when a break their way was just around the corner.

Within the context of psychology and Buddhism, we can usually assume that when we think things are under control, they're not.

I'm not suggesting that it is all just good or bad luck. The story of Duke University winning one of its NCAA basketball championships in the early 1990s is fitting. With only seconds left in the game, Duke was behind by one point. A Duke player got a defensive rebound and threw the ball full court toward the basket, but it was way short of the basket. Christian Laettner, a Duke player, was standing at the foul line and caught the ball, almost looking as if it had been passed to him. Laettner turned around and shot the ball in the basket. Just as it went through the hoop, the buzzer went off. That basket won the game for Duke. In an interview with Jim Valvano, Duke's coach, he was asked how he had coached Laettner for that play. Valvano laughed and said, You don't coach for that. But what he had coached his players to do was to always put themselves in a position to take advantage of a break if/when it occurs.

By expecting that a positive, rather than a negative, opportunity could arise at any time, we are prepared to take advantage of it when it presents itself.

Impermanence

All things lack permanence. Nothing exists the same as it did yesterday. Nor will anything be the same tomorrow as it was yesterday or today. Buddha's teaching of no-self is central to Buddhism. All things are impermanent. While human individuals and other sentient beings may resemble their past selves, they have evolved for better or worse. This impermanence is unavoidable. One major factor in this constant state of change is the principle of *dependent co-arising*. This is the change we see in ourselves and others as a result of our interactions with other humans and our environment. Nothing is static. Even our relationships change and require attention. We are either moving forward or going backward and becoming stale. A piece of stale bread is on the verge of becoming moldy and dying. A body of water will become stagnant if it doesn't have a flow of fresh water coming in and going out. As the saying goes, we never step into the same river twice.

I've had couples tell me, with sadness in their eyes, that they were essentially sidetracked by life outside their intimate relationship. They forgot to keep their relationship fresh. There is a natural ebb and flow in all relationships, marked by periods of drifting apart and reuniting. But if we don't purposefully reunite, they can drift further and further apart. A couple may be great parents to their kids or play valuable roles in their church and community. However, if they pour their total energies into being parents and the community, leaving nothing for each other, the marriage can die. There is a reason that divorce rates peak at around the twenty-first year. This is the time when kids are pulling away and are less dependent on parents, graduating from high school, going off to college, moving out and living separately, finding their life partners, and so forth. This can be a shock when parents look at each other and realize they no longer truly know each other. It's almost as if they forgot what initially attracted them to each other.

So knowing that nothing stays as it is, as it was, the couple must purposefully reconnect. Couple enrichment retreats organized by religious organizations can facilitate this reconnection. This can be especially true when one or both individuals have professional careers or jobs that they have become deeply immersed in. Weekly date nights, leaving the kids with grandparents, and getting away. The importance of these and other activities can't be overstated.

After completing my doctoral studies, I had the privilege of interning at the University of Washington's Sexual Dysfunction clinic in Seattle. The couples we saw had all been together for a while, and their primary issue was the lack of sexual satisfaction that they had had earlier in the relationship. In addition to focusing on specific parts of the sexual relationship, they were instructed to make non-sexual dates with each other each week. Each one in turn had the responsibility of planning a weekly date event together: going to dinner, cooking dinner at home, going bowling, or taking walks together for the express purpose of spending time together. It was not unusual for these couples to say that these activities, which addressed other parts of their lives than having sex with each other, were truly enriching. These activities were in addition to the homework we would assign to work specifically on their sexual relationship. As can be imagined, the twenty-plus weeks of sex therapy were pretty time-intensive. Thus, at the initial interviews, we would stress the time commitment required each week. Therefore, if they were too busy to commit this much time, we recommended that they postpone this program and get back to us when their life schedules would allow for this level of commitment.

The non-sexual part of sex therapy is essential to the success of treatment. We took each individual's sexual history about the details of their lives and strove to understand the non-sexual aspects of their relationship. We often found that they had stopped many of the behaviors they exhibited when they first met, early in their relationship. Usually, they had inadvertently let sex carry the entire weight of their intimacy. Sexual intercourse, as pleasurable as it is, can't bear that weight. It is only part of a healthy, intimate relationship.

Throughout the process of sex therapy, we continually emphasized the importance of being in the *Now*, in the moment. One of the common problems that brought couples into the clinic was that they would compare their particular sexual experiences to past times or imagined expectations, rather than just being present at this point. Many people get caught comparing a specific sexual encounter with some previous time, or with another partner, recalling how intense or incredible it was back then, or comparing it to some imagined fantasy. Remember that our fabricated memories are often more positive than they actually were.

This is one serious problem with pornography, beyond its addictive qualities. It is impossible for earthly human beings, with wrinkles and sagging muscles, to keep up with a fantasy, a fabrication. We would tell couples that there is *no scorekeeping*. Sex is also not a spectator sport. Buddhism stresses that any remembered experience is just an illusion that has most likely become exaggerated, positively or negatively: orgasms are remembered as more intense, sexual techniques remembered as almost majestic, and fireworks go off. In short, the remembered experience can be almost beyond what is humanly possible. This exaggeration, in and of itself, may have started innocently enough. However, if we use it as a standard to compare present experiences, it can cause a sense of constant failure. When one or both people get caught in this trap of comparing, significant disappointment can become the norm. This is also true when comparing experiences with another partner, especially when that other person was in the past and subject to fabrication. In the movies, fabricated magical sexual encounters are explicitly scripted. The actors are *acting* for the cameras. People who are standing around with lights are coaching. Fantasies like these can present the same problem.

So when counseling a couple through the process of sex therapy, we tell them to keep a journal handy. Once they've completed the specific assignment, or lovemaking is over, we ask them to make some particular notes. Notes about their physical and emotional responses to touching and being touched. This allows them to describe how it went at their next appointment with the therapist. We do this because details can be lost even after a couple of days.

Completing this internship was a true highlight of my young career in psychology and stands out as one of the most fortunate experiences I have had. It taught me a lot about human behavior and counseling in general.

Memories

Fish stories are a good example of exaggerated memories, often *describing the one that got away.* My son Matt and I were fly fishing on the Blue River in Colorado thirty years ago. The Blue is a beautiful river with a reputation for being a champion trout stream. We parked the car on the side of the road and made our way down to the river. The river was lined with large boulders. Matt was standing pretty high up on a large boulder and had a strike; his fly rod was bent way over, and it was a nice-sized fish. Had we been on a sandy or gravelly shore, he could have just backed up and pulled the fish onto the bank. He motioned for me to get my net while he kept the line taut so the fish couldn't slip off the hook. It was fighting in the fast water. I made my way as close to the water as possible, but I was still standing on a boulder a couple of feet above the water. When I was in position, he gradually pulled the fish to the surface, and we could see it was a big trout. I got as close as I could with the short-handled net. As I reached into the water to net the fish, I bumped the fish and it came off the hook. Matt's fly rod went slack, and we both just stared at the water for what seemed like many moments. I was afraid to even look up at him. Naturally, I felt terrible. He didn't say anything until later. He tried not to make me feel too bad about it.

Over the years, this story has come up when we are telling fish stories. Even when we aren't drinking beer. In the telling, the fish has gotten bigger and bigger, and in my mind, my ineptness in handling the net has gotten worse.

Recognizing that memories are susceptible to various distortions is a key reason why staying present in the moment, in the here and now, is crucial for maintaining healthy relationships and individual mental well-being. Even though eye witness testimony is often used in legal cases, one in three eye witness accounts is erroneous. Seventy-one percent of wrongful convictions are the result of eyewitness misidentification. This is the reason counseling emphasizes the importance of focusing on what is happening in the present. Exaggeration of past experiences is always likely.

Attributions

It's a human trait to look for explanations for things. If no reasonable explanation is apparent, Buddhism suggests that we tend to fabricate an answer to *fill in the blank*. This filling-in-the-blank is influenced by the natural inclinations of our personalities, cultural and religious beliefs, and our backgrounds, to name a few. Fundamentalist religious types fill in the blank by often attributing the cause of things they can't understand to the will of God. Conspiracy theorists usually devise theories that align with their preconceived biases. People with illusions of grandeur can be quick to take credit for good things that happen around them. Conversely, people with low self-confidence and low self-esteem are often quick to blame themselves for all the negative things occurring in their sphere. Fatalists tend to blame fate and programming. An old story is that a fatalist fell down the stairs and broke a leg. Once he was starting to get better, he said, *Well, at least that's over.* You'll often hear someone say that not being in an accident on the freeway is *the reason* they were late leaving the house.

Young children often believe they are the center of their world. As such, it is a natural part of child development for a young child to think that they are to blame for bad things happening in their immediate world, and conversely, good things are the result of being a good person. When counseling younger kids whose parents are going through a divorce, it's important to emphasize that the parents are the ones who have decided to get a divorce.

As adults, we are capable of thinking of big reasons that caused something. Especially when we don't have all the facts, this is how superstitions are formed: it must have been the black cat that ran across my path; I remember walking under a ladder. A close friend told me many years ago that they believed the reason their first child got sick and died was that he and his wife had sex before they were married. God was punishing them. Particularly when we don't have all the pertinent facts, a person can look back and find numerous reasons for something having happened. The conclusions we often draw fit what we either want to be the case, what we are afraid is the case, or what we believe about the laws of the universe. So in the case of my friend, the cause of the child's death was a congenital disability and a weakened immune system. Their explanation resulted in immense guilt and self-loathing. A medical explanation was still unfortunate, but it was without the fabricated self-condemnation.

One of my favorite research studies, which can be found in Intro Psychology textbooks, was conducted in Vancouver,

British Columbia. There is a large cable suspension bridge, the Capilano Bridge, that stretches across a broad expanse of the Fraser Canyon just north of Vancouver. The University of British Columbia conducted the study in the late 70s or early 80s. The researchers positioned attractive female students in the middle of the suspension bridge. They were instructed to stop males of similar age and ask them if they would mind answering some questions regarding the state of the government in Canada. By design, the questions were bland. After several minutes, the woman handed the man a card with her name and phone number and asked if he would mind calling her if he thought of any more information regarding the survey. Bear in mind that the Capilano suspension bridge was a couple of hundred feet above the roaring Fraser River flowing below. Because other tourists were walking by on the bridge, the bridge swayed jerkily. This swaying and being suspended above the canyon caused at least a small amount of anxiety, an increased heart rate, slight perspiration, butterflies in the stomach, and so forth.

The same attractive female students then went into Stanley Park in Vancouver. They stood on a small concrete bridge spanning a creek running through Stanley Park. They stopped the same number of males of similar age and asked if they would mind answering the same questions about the Canadian Government. At the end of the interview, they handed the men the same card with their name and phone number.

The study results showed that twice as many men interviewed on the suspension bridge called the phone number as those from the concrete bridge. And when the men called, they also asked if the women would want to meet for coffee or a drink. The study's conclusions indicated that increased mild anxiety, heightened hyper-awareness, an elevated heart rate, and slight perspiration were interpreted as signs of attraction, or chemistry, between the interviewer and the interviewee. By the way, the physical symptoms the men experienced are the same ones someone might have when they are coming down with a cold or the flu.

This study is part of a body of research literature associated with *Attributional Theory*. This theory suggests that what actually causes a situation or our reaction does not determine our response; instead, our perception of it does. Our reaction is due to what we *attribute as the cause;* that's important. So is it love or the flu?

This can be a problem when a couple engages in sexual relationships too early in the relationship. It can be challenging to tell if the emotions they are experiencing are due to the sexual relationship or due to other necessary qualities in a mature relationship, like trust, respect, and acceptance. These qualities are essential for healthy relationships over the long haul. The intensity of emotions that result from sex ebbs and flows, in addition to changing as we age.

A fifty-year-old client had been referred to me by his physician with concerns about what he referred to as an *increasing lack of sexual affection* for his wife of twenty-eight years. He had concluded that he must be falling out of love with his wife. The couple had two children who were away at college. He said he was saddened that now, at this stage in their lives, when they had more time for each other, he was not as in love as he had been fifteen years ago. His reason was that he wasn't as interested in sex as often as he had been in the past. They had sex once or twice a week. He admitted that when they did have sex, it was delightful. By comparison, when they were in their early thirties, they would often have sex at night, and sometimes wake up during the night and have sex again. Now he wasn't able to have sex several nights in succession. He still thought his wife was attractive and sexy.

I explained that as men age, our ability to get excited sexually following an orgasm gradually requires an increasing length of time. This is called a Resolution. So when a man is eighteen, he can probably get excited enough to have another orgasm in twenty minutes or so. By the time he is in his mid-thirties, it will take considerably longer. So, in his early fifties, it will probably take at least twenty-four hours. At seventy years old, it will take a few days. Therefore, the increased time it takes for him to become sexually aroused following sexual intercourse, considering his age, is normal, and is not an indication, all by itself, of a lack of love or attraction to his wife, or that something is wrong with him or their relationship.

Further, by comparing his response to the way he functioned twenty years ago, he was undercutting his ability to respond to the moment. To be in the *NOW.* Buddhism's principle of staying in the moment, free from past and future worries, helps maintain a clear understanding of our emotions and being able to accept ourselves for who we are now. Worry and its related anxiety always interfere with a person's ability to enjoy sex.

Carl Rogers, an American Psychologist in the 1940s, is responsible for an entire theory of personality and approach to counseling and psychotherapy known as *Person-Centered Theory.* The hallmark of his person-centered approach was that people are inherently capable of self-discovery. The process of self-discovery occurs when we are in an environment of acceptance, simply as we are. He emphasized the importance of clients being present in the *moment.* That anxiety, depression, and similar psychological disorders are the result of setting standards for themselves higher than who they are at this moment and during this time in their life.

Buddhism's principle of staying in the moment, free from past and future worries, is beneficial in maintaining a clear understanding of our emotions.

Absence of Essence

Emptiness is a closely related concept of Impermanence in Buddhism and is associated with the concept of co-dependent arising. The essence of who we are or what a particular occurrence means is always a fabrication. Then, what often follows is clinging to the fabrication, which stops us from continuing to grow and develop, and from looking more deeply into ourselves and others.

Because the *Now* is all we have, we are always empty, like a blank slate. As we move from moment to moment, we create our essence and then cling to it. As the fabrication settles in our minds, we use words to think about it and contemplate what that means. As soon as we label something, it becomes something other than just being in the experience. In this way, words can actually get in the way, as they become the building blocks of conscious processes. Then we become other than just *being*. It's like we become more concerned with *doing* rather than being. We judge ourselves and others on what we do, how well we do it, and how successful we are in a particular endeavor. We then use these judgments to make up our essence, which is nothing more than a fabrication.

For example, we fabricate the essence of being in a particular role, such as father, husband, wife, mother, professor, or construction worker. Over time, we come to accept fabrication as a definitive definition of who we are. This definition is usually static rather than constantly updated. In the teachings of Jesus, we are told that we are neither Jew nor Greek, bond nor free, male nor female (we are essence free)[1]. We view these judgments as on a value continuum: good or bad, better or worse.

---

1. Galatians 3:28

Additionally, these value judgements are often measured against some idealized perfection. For instance, I'm a bad parent if I get angry with my child, but I'm a good parent when my child is happy. We allow one instance to define our entire being. We tend not to give ourselves much room for error or for being imperfect human beings. A man must always be right, never wrong; a woman must be sweet and cooperative. Under these expectations, a man who gives in to a disagreement rather than arguing may be seen as weak; a woman who asserts her rights is seen as pushy, bossy, and aggressive. They don't match the imagined essences. So, essences, at best, must remain fluid and flexible.

Fabrications, developed by us, lead us to prejudice. Prejudice, thanks to natural selection, is a natural part of human behavior. We learn to *pre-judge* situations we're familiar with, so we don't have to relearn the same experience every time we're in similar situations. When driving and approaching an intersection with a stop sign, we *reflexively* take our foot off the gas and gently press the brake pedal so we can come to a complete stop. We then look for oncoming traffic to be sure it is safe to proceed. This is what we call second nature. We weren't born with this prejudice. But learning it to the extent that it's now a reflex makes it second nature. Prejudices are learned.

We internalize the fabrications that we use to fill in the gap of our knowing, and to assign the essences to others as well as ourselves. Prejudices, internalized essences, keep us from looking more deeply into ourselves and others, as well as into the rest of the world around us.

It is part of human nature to assign essences to others and to ourselves. The more importance we place on one's essence, the more we lose the ability to weigh the truth on its own merit. So we believe something just because someone in a position of authority said so: pastor, teacher, president, coach, etcetera. The hallmark of maturity is the ability to listen and think critically. When I was teaching, I tried to help my students recognize truth wherever they found it. Regardless of whether it came from someone with whom they shared many similarities and had a lot of respect, such as being a Christian, a Baptist, a Lutheran, and so on. And to avoid reflexively discounting something because the person who said it didn't have the status, in their opinion, which they had been told was important: a scholar from another culture

Emptiness is not simply nothingness, but rather, insight into the absence of essence in Co-Arising beings.[2] Paul Keenan explains that in the denial of essentialism, we are all the same—part of the same whole. In grasping and then clinging to things as if they are real, it's easy to get caught in a web of fabrication. Then, in the words of Freud, we project what we have imagined/fabricated in our mind onto others as well as onto ourselves, as if looking into a mirror. This fabrication becomes the meaning of the concepts we use to rule our lives. So Emptiness sets the stage for liberation from the illusions and imaginings of our fabrications. Granted, it is impossible to live in this complex world without encountering fabrications and preconceptions. So what do we do? We accept this in us and hold them loosely so we can let them go when we are faced with disconfirming data.

This is the value of meditation. Meditation acts like a reset, allowing us to focus on the essence we have used to construct our lives. We accept who we are and become satisfied with who we are, not who we used to be or who we hope to become. Neither the past nor the future defines the self. The self is now empty, and the essence is free.

---

2. Keenan, Paul (1989) *The Meaning of Christ: A Mahayana Theology, (pg. 133).* Orbis Books, Maryknoll, NY

Dependent Co-Arising

No sentient being is independent of itself. This is a central principle of Buddhism. The biblical scriptures reinforce the idea that we are all interdependent. An analogy of the human body illustrates this: many parts make up the body of Christ. We all have our interdependent roles to play.[3] As such, and paradoxically, we each develop individually as we interact with each other. There is no escaping being human and contingent. We can't get away from being dependent upon others as well as the environment in which we are born and in which we develop.

Our environment includes our culture and its language. First, the micro-culture, such as our immediate family, larger extended family, social environment, including our schools and churches, and so on. As well as the larger culture of media, political, and economic values. For those of us in the United States, our culture and society are a blend of democratic capitalism and democratic socialism.[4] Even though how liberally this is applied tends to ebb and flow, these values continue to undergird our societies. They influence our speech and how we think, as well as the way we view ourselves, each other, and other societies around the world.

The Middle Path of Buddhism is not merely a position of balance or moderation. It is the practice of insight into Co-Arising. Being aware of the continuing flux of existence, free from the *process* of imagining and taking on the essence to which we are so vulnerable.

---

3. 1 Corinthians 12:12-27; Romas 12:4; Proverbs 27:17; Ecclesiastes 4:9–10

4. Realizing that suggesting the U.S. has some Democratic socialist values will make many conservatives nervous, let me offer this explanation. Hopefully, this will keep you from throwing the book in the trash and failing to read further. Democratic Socialists advocate for policies like strengthening social safety nets, increasing workers' power, and expanding public services, all within a framework of a democratic political system.

Chapter Six

Early Influences: Buddha and Jesus

A Case for Integrating both Wisdoms with Psychology

As we mature in our faith and understanding of Buddha and Jesus, it helps considerably to understand that they were not just dropped onto the earth as fully developed adults ready to teach their teachings. The Buddha was born into Royalty. Siddhartha Gautama, Buddha's birth name, was the child of a king and queen. He had everything: parents, a family, a palace to live in, food, and wealth. Yet, as a young adult, he is said to have felt suffocated with discontent.[1]

The discontent with opulence and Hindu culture is what led Siddhartha Gautama to reject his privileged life as a young adult. He headed out on a pilgrimage for the remainder of his adult life, covering thousands of miles. He continued to see poverty and the inequality of life all around him. Eventually, this in turn

---

1. Tarrant, John (2024) *The Story of the Buddha,* Shambhala Publishing, Boulder, CO

resulted in his enlightenment and an ascetic lifestyle of self-denial and a focus on spiritual values,

Jesus, on the other hand, was born in a manger in a barn. His parents, Joseph and Mary, who was nine months pregnant, rode a donkey to Jerusalem to register for the census. His mother, Mary, was a young maiden, and Joseph, his earthly father, was a carpenter. When Jesus was about one year old, the young family became refugees and fled to Egypt to escape King Herod's order to kill all male children under the age of two. They stayed in Egypt until Jesus was two to seven years old. As such, as a young lad, Jesus was exposed to both Egyptian and his native Jewish cultures. As part of the Egyptian culture, Jesus was likely exposed to Buddhist thought, which had been present in Egypt for about 200 years.

From birth, we are immersed in a language that shapes how we think and develop. The primary task of adolescence and early adulthood is to sort out what we are going to do with the ideologies we have been bathed in for the first twelve to sixteen years of our lives. It's the language of our cultural origins that we use to think about these ideologies.[2] Thus, the language we are raised speaking plays a significant role in how people differ across societies and why they feel differently.

There are times when someone is translating a text from one language to another, when it's said that the original language doesn't translate precisely into the new language. So something gets lost in translation. When the Greeks incorporated the gospel of Christ into their language and, consequently, their culture, it is safe to assume that some aspects of its original meaning were lost. This is, of course, up to the experts in Hebrew and Greek to tell us for sure. When a preacher or teacher uses the phrase, *in the original Hebrew or Greek . . . ,* a word or phrase means something

---

2. The Sapir-Whorf Hypothesis

different than it was assumed to mean by those of us who were not trained in seminary to read the original. Sometimes the difference is only a nuance, other times a whole different meaning is understood. To further increase the likelihood of mistranslations, the exact words in a language can have different meanings depending on context and the historical period in which they were written. The phrase *the eye of a needle* is familiar to most of us who are familiar with the Bible. Jesus was teaching about the obstacles that extreme wealth can pose to people seeking to reach heaven. He said that it is easier for a camel to get through the eye of a needle than for a rich man to enter the kingdom of heaven. As a kid growing up in church, I considered this to be a silly, even nonsensical thing to say. Obviously, no animal can pass through the eye of a sewing needle. Thus, it had no real meaning, except that someone with wealth couldn't go to heaven—period. However, if we consider a more metaphorical meaning, referring to a very small or difficult opening to pass through, it takes on greater meaning. A small, difficult opening in the wall of a city may be possible, albeit quite tricky, for a camel to pass through. So, a more reasonable meaning might be that it is difficult for a person who possesses a deep love of money to go to heaven. Looking back on my childhood, I realize that the meaning of the 'eye of a needle' teaching was lost in translation.

Another example is 'day'. Day may mean *era,* such as *'back in my day',* or *twenty-four-hour day,* or *'it's a new day'; this is the day the Lord hath made.* A confusing point, as a youngster growing up with the literalists of the Kentucky Southern Baptist denomination, was how long it took God to create the world. Was each day a twenty-four-hour day, or an era of development? It turns out that each day was a period, thousands to millions of years, during which specific parts of the Earth came into being.

I've said all of this to make the following point. Because Jesus and his family spent at least a few years, maybe more, in Egypt, the languages and cultures Jesus was exposed to while he was in the early process of understanding who he was as a boy were probably pluralistic: Egyptian (Demotic and Greek), Jewish (Greek and Hebrew), and Buddhism which was present for at least a couple of centuries before Jesus' family living as refuges in Egypt.

Paul Keenan asserts that the Mahayana language, a significant language of Buddhism, offers a perspective that may be of value in expressing hitherto unnoticed depths of the meaning of Christ. This is precisely because it is a different language in a different culture and offers a different set of mediated insights. A different language and culture in which Jesus, his parents, and other refugees who likely lived nearby were exposed. The theology offered within Mahayana ". . . questions all systems and negates any *thought structure* that is taken to be true, . . . and moves easily with a more pluralist cultural practice.[3] Within this context, all thinking is believed to have developed in a dependent and co-arisen manner relative to particular cultural values, languages, and ways of thinking.

Mahayana Christian Theology values the wisdom teachings and insight of both traditions, Buddhist and Christian. This, therefore, significantly reduces the need for puzzlement. In other words, there is a *constant "stretching forth" of the mind toward the presence of God as Abba . . . toward the Spirit-realization of justice and peace in the concrete world.*[4]

Thus, during early adulthood, we utilize our language of origin to think through and facilitate this process. Then, in turn, we use this language to understand how we are living with the consequences of those decisions. Previous decisions always lead to further choices. This is true whether we are entering college,

---

3. Keenan, Paul, P. (1989) *The Meaning of Christ: a Mahayana Theology,* Orbis Books, Maryknoll, NY. Paul Keenan is professor emeritus of religion and an Episcopal Priest. He was also resident scholar at Nanzan Institute for Religion and Culture in Japan.

4. Ibid

pursuing a trade, joining the military, selecting a life partner, relocating to another part of the country, or even another country altogether. Language plays a crucial role in shaping how we function and think as adults.

Some have always merely gone with the flow, taken what they were handed, or some other more straightforward way, and given little if any thought to where they are headed. Further down the road of life, they are likely to face a degree of identity crisis. This is true even when the choice seemed reasonable and logical, such as attending law school to join the family law firm, pursuing a career in plumbing to follow in their dad's and uncles' footsteps, or becoming a minister to follow in their parents' footsteps. Remaining foreclosed to the values with which one was born and raised, they avoid the opportunity of owning their own beliefs and values. Think mid-life transition or even mid-life crisis. This crisis can be avoided by addressing these issues at a younger age, such as the twenties. Even if the final choice turns out to be the same, it's essential that they thought through their decision and took ownership of it.

When our two sons were in their pre-adolescent and adolescent years, I was thankful for the adults they interacted with. Those adults who had slightly or significantly different perspectives on life played a crucial role in cementing values and the early process of figuring out who they were and who they would become. These adults included coaches, teachers, youth pastors, youth group leaders, aunts, and uncles. Of course, in those early years, we felt like we had some say in who these adults were. Then they move on to college and early-career mentors whom they select as role models.

The African proverb "It takes a village to raise a child" is appropriate here and is echoed throughout the scripture. It emphasizes the crucial role a community plays in a child's development and well-being. It's so much more than just the parents.

To say this another way, we don't develop and grow in a vacuum, but in an environment of rich cross-pollination. The results of this interdependence for us, as humans, are seen in how each successive generation's members are often larger, stronger, and smarter. The impact of co-dependent arising is as strong a factor in our development as genetics. As you learned in General Psychology class, it is both nature and nurture that guide development.

Multiple factors we see around us shape who we are. Thus, we should expect to find new and expanded truths when we look in new places. As I mentioned earlier, we should expect to find new truths around the next corner, especially when we are in new surroundings. Not just in a college textbook or a church, which may only reinforce our previous learning without encouraging critical thinking.

This is why many colleges, universities, and even some high schools offer programs that allow students to study abroad for a semester, typically during their Junior or Senior year. The Council of Christian Colleges and Universities (CCCU) examined the impact that studying abroad had on students. They found that students who spent at least one semester studying in a country different from their own were much more likely to have achieved a sense of their own identity. This may or may not be something drastically different from their families of origin. However, it was their own identity, not something foreclosed by their parents. A similar impact was observed in students who attended colleges that differed from their religious backgrounds.

Truth is truth, no matter where you find it. Likewise, wisdom is wisdom is wisdom wherever it is found.

Truth is Truth

The first time this *truth-being-truth-wherever-we-find-it* dawned on me was in the mid-1970s. I was pursuing my master's degree in psychology. I was working full-time. We had two young boys. We were active in our church, and were remodeling our very old house. As such, I had gotten behind in my reading and had an essay exam coming up the following week. So I skipped church on a Sunday morning to study in a quiet house. I still have the textbook I was reading when I had this epiphany. The course was *Theories of Personality*. I don't remember the precise topic in the text. Still, I was suddenly overcome, tears running down my cheek, with the truth that what I was reading was accurate and consistent with the spiritual wisdom of Christ, even if I didn't know the scripture text that it paralleled, or even if there was an exact text that said a similar thing.

I worked at the local VA psychiatric medical center. I was working in a Behavioral Modification and Teaching Clinic (BTC). This meant that I had direct exposure to the application of psychology. This was the '70s. Some of the more severe inpatients we saw received weekly or bi-weekly Electric Convulsive Shock Therapy (ECT). This was a standard treatment for the severely mentally ill. Although I don't remember all the rationalizations for this treatment, it seemed clear that at least part of the effect was the control of the person's behavior. Seeing the actual application of the ECT left me with a sense of horror. Electrodes were placed on the patient's head, which, when turned on, would cause a seizure and physical convulsion. A large male nursing aid lay across the legs of the patients to keep them from hurting themselves when they went into convulsions. Even now, 50 years later, I can still vividly recall the scene. Many of the staff psychologists believed this treatment, administered routinely, was inhumane and similar to the chains of psychiatric hospitals of years gone by. Many of the drugs we have today had not yet been developed. So as bad as it seemed, it did serve to keep potentially violent patients subdued.[5]

---

5. Treatment plans were developed and ordered by Psychiatrists - MDs. Not PhDs

To add to this mix, I was a relatively new Christian, having been influenced by my experiences during the Vietnam War. My wife and I were part of the Jesus People in the Pacific Northwest. Even though I had taken part in the Vietnam War, I was relatively naive about spirituality and life in general. I was trying to understand my role in a Buddhist culture while in Thailand. I wanted to figure out how it all fit together, or not, with my Christian faith. While stationed at an Air Force base in Udon Thani, Thailand, I spent my spare time teaching conversational English at a trade school, making repairs at an orphanage for Thai-American babies, and hanging out at a hospitality house downtown.

Back to studying on a Sunday morning. The topic I was studying was likely related to behaviorism, a primary theoretical construct of the time. I was suddenly overcome by how true what I was reading was. Furthermore, although it would be some time before I could fully articulate it, I saw no conflict between the psychology I was learning and my spiritual self. The textbook was written for secular consumption. Although this may not seem significant today, it was a primary concern for me at the time. I could relax with who I was and absorb all that I was discovering. I could relax knowing that truth would win out, would rise to the surface.

Remaining in the Now

This co-arising process is constantly taking place from early childhood through our late years as elderly adults. This is facilitated through the integration of the wisdom of Buddha and Christ. A key attitude necessary for this absorption is staying in the *present moment, or the 'now'*. We are not who we were a while ago, the future is not here yet, so we can't predict it or count on it. In the Shambhala tradition of Buddhism, even hoping for things in the future leaves us open to disappointment or elation, an up-and-down emotional roller coaster. This leads us away from being in the now. The only thing we have is the immediate now—the here and now. Living in the present is a principle shared by Buddhism, Christianity, and psychology. As affluent Westerners, we need very little of what we accumulate. This is part of the curse of materialism. Even though I'll probably have difficulty getting rid of all of the things I have accumulated, especially my books, I know I only need a fraction of what I have.

As a psychologist, I'm not suggesting that we never discuss or reflect on past issues, nor that we should not plan for the future. Understanding how the past has impacted us can help solve ongoing problems. Therapy and counseling can be beneficial in this process when we have carried past patterns of being into our present life. However, the goal of achieving a better understanding is to eventually let the past truly become part of the past, allowing us to let go of who we were back then. The past does not define who we are *now*.

We also need to make some provisions for our future. In Western societies where we live, we must make plans for the future, including retirement, health issues, health insurance, our children's education, and so on. But we don't hold on to those plans as if they are our absolute security. Our true security, while holding on to plans loosely, is in accepting who we are at this moment in time.

By staying *in the present moment,* we embrace emptiness and become aware of co-arising. Who I am at this moment, without inherent character and essence, is a result of with whom I'm interacting. As I'm writing this, we're planning this evening's events. Phoenix, my oldest grandson, is graduating from Fire Fighter's Academy, followed by dinner at a nice restaurant. The more I'm aware of emptiness, the more I leave all the roles that I play at home. If I believe that I have to act as a grandfather, it shades how I respond to the other people present. If I need to act like a grandfather, it influences how I interact with those around me who are not my grandchildren. If I insist on acting like the wise psychologist, it interferes with how I behave with my grandkids. So I strive to attend the dinner party empty, allowing myself to respond to each individual as they are, spontaneously and without judgment. Being consciously genuine will enable me to shed the arrogance that is a part of who I am.

As we travel along the middle path of life, we are always in the presence of emptiness. Emptiness does not mean hollow or nothingness, but permits the soaking up, the co-arising from the otherness of those around me.

The more aware we are that this *emptiness and being* is the result of otherness *in the Now*, the closer I am to a heightened awakening. Even the perspectives that I understand are, in reality, nothing more than worldly conventions. Worldly convention, as limited as it is, is the avenue of horizontal social interaction. Ultimate understanding is the vertical silence that is distinct from human constructions. This Buddhist Doctrine parallels Christian doctrine, as expressed in scripture, in describing the Holy Spirit interceding for us when we don't know how to pray due to our limited understanding.[6]

We have these two truths in the wisdom of The Christ and The Buddha. Ultimate meaning requires our acceptance of the unknown, and as a result, we are unable to express it through the worldly conventions of our given languages. As stated earlier, the truths we convey through our limited understanding and the fabrications we create are always on the edge of fading into nothingness. Accepting the Ultimate knowing of unknowing is the mystical dimension of our faith, whether in Christianity,

---

6. Romans 8:26

Buddhism, or the combination of the two into a more complete whole.

Worldly Convention is always and only dependently co-arising, and as such is not directed by some divine principle.[7] So even when we offer a judgment about whether some act of compassion is worthy or not, it is made through cognitive methods and conventional insight.

---

7. Keenan, John, P (1989) *The Meaning of Christ: A Mahayana Theology,* ORBIS Books

Chapter Seven

Doctrines and Worldly Convention

Since what we are left with is our limited Worldly Convention, we develop beliefs about the ultimate knowing, which is unknowable. Therefore, we must accept that the beliefs we've created are, at best, projections of one's selfhood. The more comfortable we are with the transient nature of our beliefs in a changing world, the more enlightened we will become. This is said to be the reason that the Buddha rejected clinging to specific doctrines. He recognized that specific doctrines were the projections of the time and culture. His teachings were much more closely related to the reality in which we live and to how we respond to it. Jesus, building on where Buddha's teachings left off, also taught and lived in response to the world he inhabited. He challenged the inequities of his day. An example of Jesus' teaching is that the love of money is the root of all kinds of evil. It is difficult for a rich man to enter the kingdom of heaven. It is easier for a camel to get through the eye of a needle. Jesus stressed the need to feed and give shelter to the people who had little or nothing, to the have-nots. Except for a few of his followers, the people of Jesus' time completely missed who he was and that the Kingdom of God was in the *Now.*

He instructed them to pray that the Kingdom of God would come on earth. They missed who he was, even though they listened to him teach and looked him in the eye. A primary reason they missed him, and still do today, is that Jesus was immersed in the social and political conditions of his time. He was telling them things they weren't ready to hear, that they didn't want to hear: welcome the stranger and the refugee, sell what you have and give it to the poor, stop making money off of the gospel (money changers in the temple), build bridges with the people who are different than you (Samaritans), befriend the people who might disgust you (stop throwing stones at the woman caught in adultery). This is what got Jesus killed, and is the reason they couldn't hear what he was saying. In Buddhist terms, they were grasping and clinging to the material things of their world. By material things, I'm including the social status and power that we are drawn to, like metal flakes to a magnet. Thanks to evolution, this drawing is reflexive and becomes second nature. As such, this reflexive drawing must be addressed directly and face-on. Just wishing this were not the case is never enough.

This is achieved through increased self-awareness, fostered by practices such as mindfulness meditation, which focuses on the present moment. Meditating on the Now begins with focusing on our body, such as breathing in, breathing out, and repeating this cycle. This is the focus of relaxation training in psychology, utilizing biofeedback as mentioned earlier. Increased awareness of our bodies leads to better health by alerting us to take preventative action. In utilizing biofeedback relaxation and mindfulness meditation, physical disorders such as migraine and tension headaches, some sleep disorders, high blood pressure, and other physical problems related to stress can begin to come under conscious control. It's been said that one way to tell the difference between civilized societies and primitive societies is to look at the diseases that plague and kill their citizens. Communicable diseases kill primitive cultures. Stress-related ailments kill civilized cultures. Stress reactions become learned and second nature, reflexive. If you notice that your shoulders are tight and painful after driving in heavy traffic to work, it's because you have been unconsciously holding muscles tight. Grasping the steering wheel with a death grip is not necessary to drive. You can learn to hold onto the wheel tightly enough, but not so tightly that it increases blood pressure, causes headaches, and so on.

As we gradually become more attuned to our subtle body rhythms, we can become more aware of our presence in our physical surroundings, then to those around us and our environment. This increased awareness of others enables a more effective response to their needs.

Remember that, like Jesus, the Buddha before him was an itinerant spiritual teacher. He traveled and taught against hoarding wealth, while also advocating for sharing what they had. Buddha challenged the corruption of Vedic Priests, which was the "... cause of much of the social injustice of the day: the caste system, terrible treatment of the untouchables, and monopolization of spiritual teachings by those who enjoyed the materially lavish lifestyles, and yet were barely spiritual at all."[1]

Jesus and Buddha strove to raise awareness of societal inequities and were concerned with issues of social justice. For example, they owned only what they could carry. Most likely a bed role and a cloak.

---

1. Thich Nat Hanh, (1995) *Living Buddha Living Christ,* Riverhead Books, Division of G. P. Putnam's Sons

Social liberation today, much like in the lives of Jesus and Buddha, occurs through individuals and communities that recognize their separation from the ultimate truth. The conventional truth they possess is contextual to the present day and culture. Present-day Humanistic Psychology emphasizes the innate drive to discover one's inborn goodness and potential. Along the journey to achieving Self-Actualization, and once it's completed, we hold our grip on the process loosely. This allows us to address the needs of those around us. The hallmarks of someone who has self-actualized are their humility. Paradoxically, they are no longer concerned with self-actualization.[2] They've arrived at reclaiming one's original nature. Original goodness and grace. The highest truths of Jesus and Buddha can be understood only through faith and, in turn, through practice.

Holding lightly to fabricated doctrines

Religious dogma declares the foundational truths of the church. Although this foundation is often presumed to be fixed, permanent, and unchangeable, the expression of the dogma does change over time and is influenced by cultural progression. These changes are seen as doctrines.[3] All dogma is doctrine, but not all doctrine is dogma. Even though not all doctrine is dogma, not infrequently are doctrines expressed and preached so enthusiastically, so dogmatically that they become dogma-like over time.

After my time in the Air Force during the Vietnam War, my wife and I joined a Jesus People congregation in the Pacific

---

2. Abraham Maslow's *Hierarchy of Needs*

3. Even though I spent some time studying at a seminary and earning a Masters level certificate in Cross-Cultural Ministries, I do not consider myself to be theologically trained. So I do ask for some leeway in the use of these two terms. As you read this section try to get the intent of what I'm saying even if I incorrectly use these terms interchangeably.

Northwest. This was the early 1970s. The Jesus People movement had expanded north from California. Henri Nouwen believed that the Jesus People movement was a legitimate Christian movement. But the reason it failed to persist over time was its lack of organizational structure, which would have provided the roots needed for the longevity of religious movements.[4] Many Jesus People eventually either merged into local Christian Charismatic congregations or went their separate ways.

As part of our personal experience with the Jesus People, we mainly saw younger adults and college students searching for spiritual truths, just as we were. Many of us were from traditional Protestant and Catholic traditions. However, we were not satisfied with these traditional practices. Many Jesus People emerged from the hippie movement of the late 1960s and 1970s.

These hippie types were frustrated with the lack of response from established religions. We needed a language and doctrine that fit with the culture of the sixties and seventies. This was a time of questioning the establishment in society, in colleges and universities, in financial organizations, and in religions. The doctrines of the establishment did not fit well. The old guard, in Buddhist terms, clung too tightly to dogma and doctrines that were decades and centuries old. We needed more fluid beliefs. Times change. The sincerity of the Jesus People was expressed in a frequently heard statement of the time: they were *spiritual, but not religious*.

Christianity is facing similar challenges today and needs to respond to the needs of people in the *Present*. "Many young people all over the world have abandoned their church[es] because church leaders have not caught up with changes in society."[5] One

---

4. Henri Nouwen was a Dutch Catholic Priest. He taught in theological schools of Harvard and Yale

5. Hanh, Thich Nhat, (1995) *living Buddha Living Christ,* Riverhead Books

example of this today in the U.S. is the upheaval in conservative Christian denominations and churches over LGBTQIA2+ individuals. In many of these churches, there is a lack of acceptance by those church leaders. Over the last several years, many longtime clergy in the Church of the Nazarene (CotN) have been defrocked for their affirmation and support of LGBTQIA2+ individuals. Others have surrendered their credentials voluntarily. Many laypeople in the denomination have also left the church and joined more accepting denominations.[6] I was a member of the CotN for twenty-five years and a psychology professor at a Nazarene University for nineteen years. My wife and I also taught at an international Nazarene college in Switzerland for a period. The lack of openness to LGBTQIA2+ was one significant reason my wife and I left the Church of the Nazarene and joined the more accepting Episcopal Church.

Another ongoing example of the problem that clinging to doctrine in Christian churches is that of organizational and systemic racism. The lack of full racial and cultural integration causes a massive divide in understanding. I believe it is safe to say that the typical white church parishioner has, at best, only a superficial knowledge of the strengths and struggles of the crosstown African American church and vice versa. These divides in understanding prevent a true interconnectedness of people whose fundamental Christian beliefs are, for the most part, identical. Clinging to these cultural, political, and economic labels, which date back to the 1500s, is so very well entrenched that they continue to be just business as usual in many Christian denominations. A brief discussion of systemic racism in one Christian University can be found in my memoir.[7]

---

6. Oord, Thomas Jay & Oord, Alexa, Editors (2023) *Why the Church of the Nazarene Should be Fully LGBTQ+ Affirming,* SacraSage Press

7. Henning, Douglas, (2024) *From There to Here: Many Threads of Deconstruction,* SacraSage Press

This clinging to outdated, and even evil, doctrines is part of my attraction to Buddhism. That the past is always the past, and the future is not here yet. So the only thing we have is the now. This is despite how firmly entrenched those old doctrines are. Emphasizing this highlights the importance of being present in the *Moment.* When we are awakened to certain irrelevant and harmful practices and beliefs from the past, we need to release them. This is necessary so we can truly be in the now. By doing this, we can help stop the pain caused by those doctrines. The happiness that accompanies this letting go allows us to benefit from the interconnectedness we share with all people. Digging deeply into Buddhism has been a guide back to my roots in Christ. This has allowed me to realize, for the first time in a long time, and understand the value of relationships with other human and sentient beings—all of creation. No one is an island. Not even one who has taken a particular pride in being self-sufficient.

Individualism's Curse

The doctrine of *individualism* is deeply ingrained in our capitalist culture. Admittedly, it does have some benefits, such as achievements in science and medicine, to name two areas. It also has a significant downside in the isolation it causes. We often fall into the trap of believing that we don't need each other. This is true as a nation and as individuals. As I write this, it has become an almost daily occurrence to hear, out of our arrogance, that our present administration is cutting ties with other nations and long-time allies. We have long rushed to war in attempts to punish other countries into submission and into the ways we want them to behave. To bow down to our every move. The evidence of the tyranny of individualism is a significant contributor to our personal loneliness and cultural isolation. We were not created to live in silos. That we are made for fellowship is a frequent theme in spiritual formation.

We must heed the Buddhist teachings of emptiness, nonself, and interbeing. Our being is not our own. We belong to each other, to our ancestors, to our loved ones, neighbors, future generations, and all other living beings. When we travel within the U.S. and abroad, it is always impressed on me just how much people we've never met are a part of us. These human beings may, at first glance, appear to have very little in common with us: different colors, different body shapes and sizes, different traditions and beliefs, and so on. And how much richer our lives are because of our interactions with them. It's been said that one way to reduce prejudice and bigotry is for people with diverse backgrounds and experiences to work and live together. This is how we begin to see others as kin, relatives, brothers, and sisters. This is why we are created. For fellowship with God as well as each other, with the God we see in the other.

We are made with a need that only interactions with others can fill. This is why social isolation, like solitary confinement in prison and exile, is used as an ultimate punishment. This is what the Buddha's teachings were intended to convey. The growth we experience throughout our lives is facilitated by dependent co-arising. We are the result of the interactions with the world around us. Psychologist Erik Erikson's theory of the Psychosocial stages of human development speaks directly to this. This inner being is not just a characteristic of our growing-up years, but is a part of our being that continues throughout our lives. The non-self principle of Buddhism exists in our emptiness, which receives the interactions we have with other humans and all sentient beings. This is the reason that no permanent essence of self exists. It's constantly changing in response to the ever-changing surroundings we exist in. The five aggregates of the elements of consciousness continually interact with one another:

consciousness, form (awareness of our physical body), feelings/emotions, perception, and mental formation (volition). This constant interaction is the mind's energy and is therefore never the same from one moment to the next.

It is through this constant interaction that we are shaped throughout our lives. C.S. Lewis and R.R. Tolkien were members of The Inklings, a group of writers from Oxford who met regularly for encouragement and criticism of each other's writing projects. When one of the members died, Lewis said he would not only miss the presence and that specific friendship of the deceased member, but also what that man could bring out in the others. No one else could bring out the same things that he could.[8] The unique characteristics within us, which result from interactions with other humans and sentient beings, contribute to the constantly changing self.

Even when we are asleep, there is ongoing brain activity, including dreaming. During Rapid Eye Movement (REM) sleep, the brain is processing, as observed in sleep studies. Several years ago, I came across a research article that likened dreaming to a computer when it's offline and processing. When laboratory animals are deprived of dreaming during sleep, they struggle to remember the new tasks they learned that day, such as running a complex maze. Dreaming involves categorizing new experiences in our minds.

As a personal note, I can say with Thich Nhat Hanh, ". . . that I do not feel any conflict within me." [Regarding this combination of Christianity and Buddhism.] ". . . instead I feel stronger because I have more than one root" [anchor]. The reason is that we have experienced two sources of wisdom and awakening, which date back more than two thousand years. Add to this the

---

8. Glyer, Diana Pavlac (2007) *The Company They Keep: C. S. Lewis and R. R. Tolkien as Writers in Community*, The Kent State University Press, Kent, Ohio

depth that two hundred years of evolving psychology brings in understanding human behavior, and we have several sources of wisdom to guide us. These sources offer different lenses through which to view ourselves and understand the world we live in. They serve as checks and balances. One hour becomes the next hour, and the day of this morning changes into the day of this afternoon. Some of what we thought was true falls away as a natural part of growth and development. Other antiquated truths are pruned away. Nothing is ever wasted. Everything has served a purpose to get us where we are today. Since we are always new, we don't need to be weighed down with old insights that are no longer useful. When we grasp and cling to the old chaff, it's like gathering up all the chaff and continuing to carry it with us. Allowing the chaff to be blown away by the winds of growth leaves us with new grains of wheat. Imagine how painful and burdensome it would be if we insisted, through grasping and clinging, on dragging along the past branches that have been pruned away, just like the snake that sheds its old skin and leaves it behind to become food for worms and compost for bushes. We need to let the past die off and fall away.

Ideas from yesterday can become illusions and quickly turn into idols in our minds. Even ideas of the way we think Jesus was in the past can be idols. We tend to idolize past spiritual experiences and worship their memory. A central premise of Buddhism is that the past is gone, completely gone, and that the only thing we have today is the present moment, or the *Now*. If we hold up illusions and fabrications of past events as a standard we need to get back to, we are bound for failure. This is the reasoning behind stressing the importance of sexual relationships, as not trying to compete with the past. The present reality cannot possibly compete with a fantasy. In Jesus and Buddha, new birth, being born again, is always now.

Carl Rogers' *Person-Centered* counseling emphasizes the importance of setting standards of who we are in the present moment. Anxiety and depression are, in Roger's view, the result of trying to measure up to some artificial standard of behavior that is set by anyone other than ourselves. When we allow an external standard to guide us, it is often not grounded in reality. Especially when the source of that standard of being, which we're striving to achieve, comes from a fabrication based on some memory, or fantasy, or competition with others, or with some impossible expectation for the future.

We must understand that even the presence of God is a mental construct and not amenable to our conscious understanding. From several years ago, the *death of God* presumption was not so much a factual statement of a divine deity, but that an objective God was meaningless. To objectify God doesn't matter any longer.[9] In fact, clinging to that idea only gets in the way of our spirituality in the present moment. Acceptance of this is excellent news. Since conditions are constantly changing, we don't have to go back and re-fabricate our illusions of God. This allows God to be in us and in others with whom we are dependently co-arising. It's this Buddha Nature, the potential to be awakened, which is in all of us, that allows for this enlightenment, this awareness.

Again, I'm not suggesting that we never have to process and sort out our past. Particularly when we've held on to the past and dragged it forward into the present. We often bring past fears, regrets, and should-haves with us and cling to them. According to the Buddha's teachings, this causes pain and suffering. One example from the Old Testament illustrates how we may need to confront our fears directly. Elijah is fleeing in fear from Queen

---

9. Keenan, John, P. (1989) *The Meaning of Christ: A Mahayana Theology,* Orbis Books, Maryknoll, NY

Jezebel, who has vowed to kill him. He's running into the desert and hiding in a cave. Elijah tells God that, in addition to running for his life, he is tired of being alone as a prophet. You can almost hear Elijah's panic. Then, as God begins talking to Elijah, he finally calms down so he can understand what God is saying. God tells him not to be distracted by all the spectacular events happening, such as earthquakes, landslides, and fires. As God begins talking in a reassuring, gentle voice, Elijah lays out all of his fears. He then tells Elijah that he wants him to return to the wilderness, just as he came. When he returns, after he has done a few prophet-like jobs, God will anoint another prophet in his place.[10]

It wasn't that the fire, earthquakes, and landslides were unimportant. But Elijah had worked himself into such a panic, fearing for his life from Queen Jezebel, that he got distracted by natural occurrences. So much so that he couldn't focus on what God was saying to him. It's natural to be concerned about natural forces such as these: intense windstorms, fire, and earthquakes. But his concern was out of proportion and turned into fear. This level of fear, or anxiety, does nothing to help cope. In this case, Elijah had dragged his fears and apprehensions with him into the present. Once he calmed himself, he could focus on what needed to be done in the *Now*. Practicing mindfulness meditation regularly can have this same effect.

Ultimately, it has little to do with the actual words we use to think about God. But it does have to do with the fluidity of our understanding. If we cling to old, worn-out explanations of God, Jesus, the Holy Spirit, and Buddha, it is a sure bet that we will miss God. God will move on, has moved on. Having spent the vast majority of my life in and around religious organizations and groups, I know how easy it is for us to get sidetracked. We

---

10. 1 Kings 19: 10-21

get sidetracked on wordy tangents using "yeah, but" excuses for not moving forward on this or that. A pastor friend used to say that "yeah-buts live in the woods" and don't help us solve this or that issue.

I'm not in the least suggesting that being involved in a local Christian congregation or Buddhist meditation center is fruitless. Our involvement is crucial to the continual co-arising of ourselves and others. However, the emphasis placed by those communities must be on *Now;* on allowing, even encouraging, us to de-fabricate the spiritual illusions to which we have grasped and are clinging to. Those illusions we have grasped onto as if our concepts of our mindful Buddhist Nature, our mindful Spirit of God, were concretely and ultimately holy in and of themselves. Our imagined concepts are only transient because they are based on conventional truths. As Keenan points out, our language must be a constant *stretching forth* toward the presence of God. Toward the Spirit-realization of justice and peace in our concrete world.[11]

---

11. Ibid

Chapter Eight

Problems with Words and Concepts

The Buddha cautioned against excessive words and discussion, especially about the ultimate truth, which is beyond our understanding in the first place. Philosophizing and spending ink on ideas always springs from a conventional wisdom that will eventually change as cultures change and adapt to new developments. Theologians spend a lot of time discussing and writing about traditional views of God. Entire careers based on religious beliefs are focused on these conventions. Since we don't have a clear understanding of the ultimate truth anyway, Buddha did not want his disciples to engage in these activities. He wanted them to be doing what was much more critical: addressing the needs of people on the margins who needed shelter and food. Those who had been victims of injustice and inequality. In short, the social justice issues of the day. James, in the New Testament, echoes Buddha's thoughts almost verbatim: *faith without works is dead.*[1] Faith must be accompanied by motivated action and

---

1. James 2:26.

a sense of purpose. Christians who engage in the faith versus works debate, as if one is more important than the other, risk completely missing the point. It is not an either-or issue. It's both.

My religious roots come from conservative, fundamentalist, and literalist Christianity, which looked down its collective nose at social programs in the church, calling it a "social gospel". It wasn't just that it was a lower form of the gospel in their opinion, but not a part of the gospel at all. When I returned to school after my stint in the Vietnam War, Joyce and our two young boys were living hand-to-mouth. Our very kind Mormon neighbors were quick to include us in their church's food bank program and regularly brought us food. This was despite the fact that we were not Mormon. I was impressed with their willingness to address our social needs.

Thich Nhat Hanh cites philosopher Ludwig Wittgenstein, "Concerning that which cannot be talked about, we should say nothing." We need to abandon our habit of perceiving everything through concepts and representations.[2] This can make those of us who have spent significant portions of our lives in intellectual pursuits, such as academics, nervous. We enjoy and find comfort getting lost in our heads, playing with and debating ideas and concepts. Paradoxically, in psychology, we recognize this intellectualizing as a defense mechanism. *Intellectualization* is a way of avoiding emotional engagement. It's a way of putting emotional distance between ourselves and others. Intellectualizing to the extreme is the process of getting sidetracked by facts and details, often leading to a loss of focus. Some Christian religious communities avoid, at all costs, dealing with the more mystical and emotional side of their faith. This was the point earlier in the book about the problem in early Christianity of the Greeks

---

2. Hahn, Nhat Nhat (1995) *Living Buddha Living Christ* page 138, Riverhead Books, NY, NY

hijacking Jesus' teachings. The benefit of the Tibetan language of Mahayana Buddhism cautions against too many words. Words get in the way. Intellectualizing keeps us from understanding the other part of how our brain works. It also prevents us from understanding at a deeper level what is being experienced by ourselves and the other person. In recent years, this has been referred to as emotional intelligence.

I used to see this when doing couples and marriage counseling, where one resists getting "too emotional"—or saying that they would be happy to change something if the other could give them some factual reasons for doing so.

They would argue that making a change without a logical reason doesn't make sense to them. Rather than being willing to work on something simply because the other person says that a particular behavior bothers them. In heterosexual relationships, this is often the man who is uncomfortable primarily trusting just their partner's emotion, and refuses to talk about something unless they can reason it out. Rational-Emotive Behavior Therapy (REBT)[3] attempts to help people understand that there are two primary ways of thinking and problem-solving: intellectual reasoning and emotional reasoning. In reality, of course, we all use a combination of the two. Goals in couples therapy include helping partners accept and understand each other's primary mode of experiencing, rather than discounting the way they're not accustomed to relating. Reaching the more profound truth requires the willingness to suspend superficial and conventional understandings. One partner may find themselves saying that they don't understand what their partner is saying or what they want. Often, men hide behind what they *say* is logic, using the defense mechanism of intellectualization. What is logical

---

3. Albert Ellis is the originator of this type of Cognitive Behavior Therapy. Aaron Beck is another pioneer in Cognitive Behavior.

to them? In reality, the logic they are referring to is composed of conventional, circular nonsense. So since their mate isn't as well-versed in B.S, their *logical language,* they refuse to talk any longer. Words can get in the way and serve as a roadblock to a healthier relationship.

Learning and practicing mindful meditation provides a specific, purposeful way of being that is free from words and thoughts. Admittedly, our minds wander, and thoughts intrude. But these are only thoughts—energy of the mind. By labeling these thoughts as random and returning to focusing on your breathing, you can become accustomed to being without them for more extended periods. This is when meditation becomes a peaceful and calming experience.

Knowing that words can easily get in the way, we must use our words carefully. We speak with care so that our listeners don't get mired in those words and concepts and miss the importance of action. As the saying goes, the walk should match the talk. In human communication, words convey only around 7% of what is communicated. The other 93% comes from nonverbal cues, such as tone of voice and body language. So again, although words are important, the bulk of communication comes from somewhere else. A person can say one thing but mean another. Similarly, our daily lifestyle reveals who we truly are and what our true priorities are. Words do add an element of clarity, helping ensure our actions are understood. In the book of Matthew, we're instructed not to be like the hypocrites who like to pray publicly in a loud voice so that people will hear them.[4] Our prayers and meditations need to be done in quiet and in private. When our actions match our words, we are touching both the living Christ and the living Buddha.

———————————

4. Matthew 6:5

When observing how people in healthy, committed relationships relate to each other, we expect to see consistency between their verbal and nonverbal behaviors. If one person claims to respect and love the other, but is not considerate of the other's feelings and needs, it raises questions about their sincerity. When the two don't match, the nonverbal behavior is usually believed.

Eternal Life

The concept of eternal life, I was taught as a youngster, started when we died and went to heaven to be with God and Jesus. When someone died, people would say, as a way to comfort themselves and others, *that so-and-so is in a better place, with Jesus, in heaven.* The implication is that until we die, we are not in heaven, not with Jesus. When we reach heaven, eternal life begins. This contradiction in terms is almost humorous. By definition, eternity must already have begun and merely encompasses our brief time on earth. So, when does eternity start, or for that matter, when does it end? In Buddhist thought, there is no beginning, no end, no coming, no going, for that matter, no birth, no death. It's all a continuous process. It's eternal. Similarly, in Christian thought, it's all eternal. Our time on earth is just a part of eternity. Heaven, Eternity, Nirvana is *Now.* So what is eternity going to be like for you, for me? Is it just going to be a continuation of what is Now? I think so.

This is, at least in part, the reason for the emphasis on living in the *Present Moment* in Buddhism and Christianity. How we behave from this moment to the next is an expression of my eternal being—feeding the hungry, caring for the needy, and the sick. Jesus told his disciples that when he was hungry, they fed him, when he was naked, they clothed him, and so on—showing compassion to all sentient beings. Challenging inequity, striving for fairness, ending *Us Vs Them.* It's all *Us.* And growth in this context is available all the time, twenty-four-seven. Each moment is a moment of renewal. The compassion and loving kindness of Jesus, the Enlightenment of the Buddha, and his concern for issues of inequity and social justice continue to grow every day. Every time we respond to Jesus' teachings by attending to one another's needs, we are living a deeply spiritual existence.

Finding Wisdom

Earlier references to truth being truth wherever we find it, and wisdom being the same, provide comfort in the pursuit of knowledge. Several Bible scriptures state that those who seek will see God. This seeking and finding doesn't seem to discuss specific paths in the process of seeking. But it's the process of seeking that leads to the finding.

Buddhism and Christianity are ongoing revelations. The New Testament refers to progressing from glory to glory,[5] which suggests a continuing process of spiritual growth. The writer of Hebrews chides the readers for not having grown beyond an elementary level of maturity and says that they should be teachers and preachers by this time in their lives. Buddhism approaches this from a different angle, reminding us that the only thing we truly have is the present moment, or the *Now*. The suggestion being that the past has no bearing on us, it should no longer influence us. Clinging to what we were even yesterday is the primary cause of pain in this life.

Many psychological theories emphasize the importance of being present. Dwelling in or rehashing the past beyond the purpose of understanding and breaking free of it keeps us stuck in old habit patterns. Once we've sorted out the past and developed new patterns of behaving and relating, it's time for growth—for

---

5. 2 Corinthians 3;18

moving toward self-actualization and reaching one's true potential. Granted, this may well be like peeling an onion, one layer at a time. As we mature through one stage of life to the next, we may need to **address some past issues *now* that we have a stronger sense of self and greater** maturity.

An example is that of a child who was sexually abused at the age of five years old. At five, the goal of therapy is to help her know that she is safe and not in danger of future abuse. Then, as she is entering pre-adolescence, she will probably need to sort through that trauma with the newer level of cognitive understanding which comes with being eleven or twelve, then again as she is in the early stage of puberty. And again, as she enters young adulthood and so forth. Needing to revisit this trauma at different stages of development is not a simple rehashing, but dealing with things at a more profound level. It's part of healthy human nature to progress through more profound revelations as we age.

For the last ten years of my professional career, I operated a psychology office in an Internal Medicine Residency health clinic affiliated with a medical school. Some of my clients were medical students. These college graduates were now learning to care for people's physical needs. As such, they were investing themselves in their patients' lives at a fairly intimate level. Occasionally, this would trigger some personal traumatic issues from the medical student's past, which they thought they had already sorted out. In actuality, they had sorted out those issues at the level they were at. But this new level of dealing intimately with people, who had placed their trust in them, brought to the surface deeper levels of their trauma with which they now needed to work through.

Jesus and Buddha, although they lived several hundred years apart, exemplified the process of spiritual and social growth through their wisdom. As they grew into young adults, dependent co-arising within their respective cultures, they became increasingly aware of the social inequities affecting the people with whom they interacted. In this process, they developed positive interactions that would mark their lives of service: treating others with acceptance, kindness, respect, and love in every interaction.

For Jesus, the emphasis was on treating all people with loving kindness, while challenging the political inequities that oppressed the people, which eventually got him crucified. He personally distanced himself from the church and political leaders of his time. No doubt these leaders felt self-conscious about their lack of respect and love, as well as their own hypocrisy. It's been said that if Buddha had lived during the same time as Jesus, Buddha would have likely been put to death as well.

Learning and developing wisdom through the lives of the Buddha and Christ, as well as through Buddhism and Christianity, requires the ability to tolerate ambiguity. Developing this tolerance can occur naturally as part of human cognitive development. As discussed earlier in Fowler's stages of spiritual growth, the ability to tolerate ambiguity is a higher-order intellectual function. This cognitive ability, referred to as formal operations, begins to manifest itself in later adolescence and young adulthood. This is a change from the concrete functions of childhood and pre-adolescence. At first, it may be tempting to view this tolerance for ambiguity that we have achieved as an improvement over our previous state. Yet, Fowler stresses that, in many ways, this is just a *different* way of processing. Some adults never reach this level of thinking—the ability to think in terms of *what-if* and *'I don't know for sure'* levels of mental processing.

Embracing wisdom from sources different from the belief system in which one was raised or indoctrinated requires this tolerance for ambiguity. This is especially true if other sources of wisdom have been viewed as antagonistic in the past. At this point in my journey, it is reasonable to interpret the teachings of Christ and Buddha as being compatible. Thich Nhat Hanh says that he doesn't see *that much difference between Christians and Buddhists. . . . most of the boundaries we have created are artificial. Truth* [and wisdom] *has no boundaries. . . . Our differences may be primarily in emphasis.*[6] I agree! In addition to these two wisdoms is the cultural interweaving of contemporary psychological theories. Wisdom is more complete when it draws from multiple sources of truth, as well as allowing the excess baggage of the chaff, which has been dragged along over the centuries, to be blown away by the wind of critical thinking.

An example of the chaff I'm referring to has to do with the notions consistent with so many exclusionary religious doctrines, such as the lines drawn in the sand only a few hundred years ago, prohibiting people of particular races from worshiping with white people of European descent, or demanding that American Indians become Christian, and outlawing their centuries-old religious beliefs. Indian children were kidnapped and taken to be educated in Christian boarding schools. There are adults alive today who suffered under this evil. Sadly, it is not that difficult to find communities of people who still believe in these boundaries, despite their evil nature. Seeking to erase the details of slavery and other abuses so that white people are not uncomfortable with their own heritages is a continuation of these practices. In today's vernacular, several states have outlawed specific curricula that are consistent with being 'woke'—a term that refers to being awakened. The sin of history repeating itself when we know better is unpardonable. All of this also applies to the decisions of some longstanding Christian denominations to shun LGBTQA+ individuals from membership and prohibit them from leadership. The immoral practices of treating people

---

6. Hanh, Thich Nhat (1995) *Living Buddha Living Christ,* pg 154, Riverhead Books

in this manner are shameful and un-Godly, and show a complete lack of wisdom within the political and religious systems that support them.

The lack of compassion and wisdom described here is evidence enough that our Western political and Christianized systems do not contain *all* truths and values. A significant part of the problem is that our beliefs about ultimate reality, the Kingdom of God, and Buddhism's awakening are based entirely on conventional wisdom. This wisdom is culturally bound to the time in which it was written and preached. We need to understand that cultural relativity is a problem that we must address. Something might have been relevant a hundred years ago or two thousand years ago, but is no longer appropriate today. Wisdom is required to bravely seek truth, that while it may have been historically relevant, is no longer true. Primarily, when the *truth* was initially based only on convention, as all writings were. A case in point has to do with homosexuality. The original prohibitions originated from Jewish law, as outlined in the Talmud. Yet many Jewish prohibitions concerning other issues have long been recognized as antiquated and assumed not to be relevant for today, such as women's roles in the church, including teaching and instructing men; the eating of Kosher food; and blood oaths in seeking revenge, such as an eye for an eye. The reason for these and other shifts is that the conventional wisdom of that time is no longer appropriate. Today, some denominations and theologians specifically affirm LGBTQA+ individuals, and Reform Judaism and Conservative Judaism have followed suit.

As Jewish theologian Abraham Heschel once said, if we intend *to live the life of eternity within time,* within a historical framework, and hopefully touch the ultimate dimension, *we talk too much about it.* In Zen tradition, we need to talk less and experience it more.

Chapter Nine

Concluding Thoughts ———————

A Tapestry

As I mentioned in the section on communication, when behavior and actions do not align with the talk, we at the very least miscommunicate and confuse. But what is often true is that all we do is talk about it. We don't attempt to walk a little way down that path. The walk doesn't match the talk. This was repeatedly what Jesus took issue with. The hypocrites speak loudly to be heard, but do not feed the hungry, take care of the sick, shelter the homeless, and continue to snub the inclusion of people on the margins of society.

If being very concerned about this makes me woke, please count me in. That's a compliment. Both Christ and the Buddha took issue with this. Beginning with my time in the Vietnam War while living in Thailand, I was bothered by a general lack of civility toward the people of the world who are not white, not of European descent, and by the luck of birth, not affluent by Capitalistic standards. I know that this existed long before our current political leaders. The apparent lack of concern that we display as a nation for these and other social issues, including many conservative religious leaders, is what Jesus and Buddha preached against. These attitudes were used to justify slavery from the 1500s. Sadly, it's become ingrained in our social DNA in the U.S.

One of the things that attracted me to the field of Psychology was the belief, albeit somewhat naive, that it was possible to alleviate, or at least lessen, human psychological and emotional suffering. We needed to inform and educate people on thinking more positively about themselves and treating one another better. I like to think that I've accomplished a measure of this with some of the people I've had as clients and students in my classes. I still believe that psychology can serve as a common denominator. Its focus is to make life better for everyone, to help communities get along more effectively, and to be kind to one another. Fifty years ago, a significant divide existed between conservative religious organizations and the field of psychology. Both sides fueled this divide. Many schools of psychology saw religion as a crutch and as enabling dysfunction. And particularly conservative religions believed that psychology aimed at discrediting religion and saving people from it.

I was doing my doctoral studies at a large secular state university in the early 1980s. We were attending a conservative Christian church. More than once, members of the church would ask if I was a Christian when I started my career and studies in psychology. As we talked, it became clear they felt sad for me that I had invested so much time and energy into the study of psychology, and now I was a Christian. They expressed puzzlement when I told them that I had been a Christian for many years before I began working and studying psychology. I often said that I felt more accepted by my fellow doctoral students and professors of my Christian faith than I did by my fellow conservative church members in my psychology.

Today, there is greater acceptance of one another on both sides. When questions of religious beliefs arose in the counseling office, I would tread lightly at first. I'd want to know whether the person belonged to a congregation and felt comfortable with the pastor, Rabbi, Imam, or Monk. When this was the case, I sometimes helped them think through ways to talk with these religious leaders about their spiritual concerns. I felt it was vital for me to be the psychologist, rather than a spiritual mentor, in my clients' lives. Of course, this was not always an easy distinction to make when a person's religious beliefs, or specific religious community, were contributing to their mental health or relationship issues. In the mid-1990s, I presented a paper at an APA conference on psychologists and ministers seeing each other as collaborating professionals in local communities. The paper was warmly received by those in attendance, mostly psychologists.

Psychology's emphasis on mental health can help bridge some of the differences among religions and between faith and psychology by focusing on specific behavioral and emotional needs. All faiths share certain commonalities. But it is easy to get stuck focusing on theological differences, which stalls efforts to cooperate on the things we have in common: feeding the hungry, adequate healthcare and housing, and figuring out how to address the problems around immigration rather than just closing our gates and sending people away because we don't want to, or don't know how, to share what we have.

There are mental health organizations that are effective advocates for change at the local and national levels. However, due to the political tendency to avoid funding what is perceived as preventive programs, the necessary funding is often unavailable at the required level. For instance, our violent and gun-infested society is a significant problem. When there is a shooting, we hear about thoughts and prayers, and then politicians quickly grab onto and cling to money, which funds their pet projects and pays their salaries. I don't recall ever hearing anyone in a position of influence say they'd be willing to forgo their pet project to funnel funding toward research and prevention. Instead, a lot of talk, talk, talk, is spent about ". . . it's a mental health issue and we just need to keep guns out of the hands of people with mental illness." Then we either cut funding for mental health care or fail to advocate for real change adequately. And we resist doing adequate background checks to keep the guns out of the wrong hands. Talk is cheap. Words get in the way.

There needs to be changes in our collective souls, our spirits, our minds. Jesus spent *his life* attempting to convince individuals, his followers, and the religious and political elites of these social problems two thousand years ago, and to behave more civilly toward one another. Before him, the Buddha spent his entire life teaching and discipling his followers in kinder, peaceful ways to *BE*. He stressed the need to limit how much we talk about these things and to start being and doing.

From my time during the Vietnam War, living in Southeast Asia with some of the world's poorest people, I saw people who appeared to be much more focused on peace and living peacefully. When my wife and I returned to South East Asia in 2019 for a month, we were both struck by the same kindness and gentleness of its people.

A combination of Christianity and Buddhism, as described in this book, has a great deal to offer the world, and incorporating psychology and a concern for social justice can serve as a calming factor in this convergence. This combination makes great sense both cognitively and spiritually. However, if I had to pick one over the other, I'd say that the core beliefs of Buddhism have more to offer the world than much of the conservative brand of religions we see around the world. I realize that I'm jaded by the way Christianity is practiced in White Western society. I've had enough of all the talk. Buddha's emphasis on less talk and more action makes a lot of sense.

Here's the good news. When someone has tired of an old way of looking at things, of searching for truth and wisdom, it turns out we can take another path up the mountain. For Christians, Buddhism can shed light on Christ and his teachings of proper behavior, causing old wisdom to shine as if newly found. For Buddhists, the converse is also true. When psychology is the chosen path, our goal is to develop wisdom in our current and specific situations, with the hope that this newly acquired wisdom will also apply to our broader world. Also, we've all had the experience of an ah-ha moment when we suddenly have an insight into this or that. This is the way truth and wisdom work when we operate from a position of openness and curiosity. Embracing the new wisdom and finding avenues for application is essential, rather than letting this new awareness drift into just another fleeting experience.

The analogy of the confluence of three mountain rivers into one larger river is helpful here. Each of the three smaller rivers of wisdom, as they journeyed toward a common meeting point, sought to reach the point of confluence. Each came from a different, but similar point of origin, with the same goal of finding broader wisdom and making their own contribution to the larger whole. So we could have taken any one of the three to get to the destination. This is excellent news. We didn't have to worry that we might be on the wrong river, or in Buddhist talk, on the wrong *path*. All three are different, but they lead in the same direction to the same destination.

It's the actively seeking that is crucial. It's common knowledge to those of us who have spent any time in the mountains. If you get lost, find a stream and follow it. It will eventually lead you out. The Christian scriptures contain numerous passages that promise the seeker they will see God.[1] Buddhist scriptures promise the same, that the seeker will become Awakened.

Hopefully, the reader has been persuaded that a measure of the *Confluence of Buddhism, Christianity, and Psychology* is a helpful way to seek wisdom. We don't have to limit our path to just one of them individually. We can rely on any combination of the two or three.

I offer you the following approach. Be willing to dig deeper into each of these, looking objectively. Do this rather than rejecting a new perspective because of some old illusions and fabrications based on conventional reasons. Don't let others think for you. A friend from back in the Jesus People days said that he admittedly didn't know anything about Buddhism, but he absolutely could not understand what a person's teaching who had been dead for more than two thousand years had to offer me. He must have overlooked the fact that the writers of the Bible have been around for 2000 plus years, too. Although I imagine he meant well, he was unwilling to do any study to try to understand Buddhism.

Conversely, be willing to critically question old assumptions. Challenge religious authorities and buck traditional wisdom. Buddha expressed doubt about what he had been taught as a child and eventually abandoned the assumptions he had been raised under. This became a part of his lifestyle. At the age of twelve, Jesus was sitting among the teachers of the Jewish law in the temple, listening and questioning. Both of these men made a habit of questioning everything. This is a model for us as seekers of wisdom, *built on doubt, skepticism, experimentation, and*

---

1. Deuteronomy 4:29, those who seek God with their whole heart will find Him; Proverbs 8:17, "I love those who love me, and those who seek me diligently will find me"; Psalm 105:4 encourages believers to seek the Lord and His strength, and His presence continually.

individual responsibility.[2] This is especially true when a teacher is in a position of respect and authority. Buddha and Jesus both taught that we must think for ourselves and not be swayed by persuasive speech. I attempted to do this with my students as well as my clients and patients. If they believed what I said simply because I said it or because they read it in a textbook, it was worth very little. They would be just as easily talked out of it. If I could persuade them, someone else would come along and convince them of something else. Truths need to be owned by the individual, not borrowed from one's parents, teachers, preachers, or monks. Thinking for oneself should be the end goal of all education. Merely reciting back information in a mode of foreclosure may help you answer questions correctly for a better grade on a test. But remaining foreclosed in your cognitive reasoning is what eventually leads to identity and midlife crises.

It's essential to view the scriptures of both Buddhism and Christianity as stories about how God is with humanity. Neither Buddhist scriptures nor Christian scriptures are factual reports like the nightly breaking news. These scriptures were written down by different authors from different geographical regions at various times, sometimes a few hundred years apart. This is the very reason that inconsistencies appear within the covers of these texts. The discrepancies should push us to look more deeply for meaning beneath cultural accounts. I heard Christian author Juan Carlos Ortiz say many years ago that the Bible is intended to be like a flashlight. It guides us on our path ahead. The Bible is not supposed to be a light that we shine in our own and others' eyes that shields us from the path we are walking.

We don't have to look far inside the Christian faith to see many, many different interpretations of what is meant by a

---

2. Salguero, Pierce, C. (2022) *Buddhish: A Guide to the 20 Most Important Buddhist ideas for the Curious and Skeptical,* Beacon Press, Boston

particular scriptural source. From ultra conservative literalists who believe in a six-thousand-year earth, to the ultra liberal. From a white supremacist gospel used to justify slavery from the 1500s to present-day bigotry and national isolationism. Buddhism suffers from the same issues. There are literalist fundamentalist Buddhists who engage in proselytizing because they believe their way is the only way. At the other end of the continuum is the Modern Secular Buddhist, who views the Buddha more as a scientist or psychologist. These Buddhists believe the Buddhist scriptures accurately describe how the mind works, and that Awakening is the natural result of practicing Buddhist techniques.[3]

Given these extreme differences between groups that each believes are correct, what are we to do when deciphering true wisdom as we live in today's world? For Buddhism, Christianity, and Psychology, I have taken the approach over the last fifty years to assess, as much as possible, each point and sub-philosophy as it stands on its own, without allowing what I think others will think about it. If it has validity in its own right, I then consider its place in my own thinking. I encourage you, the reader, to do the same.

Here's a suggestion on how to approach something new. When some wisdom makes sense, but you're not sure how it may fit with other perspectives that you hold, put it on the back burner for a while. Let it simmer rather than throwing it out. Then look at it again later. You may need to repeat this from time to time. One of two things will happen. At some point, you may see that what has been on the back burner has boiled away and is no longer there. Or, as in my own experiences, simmering allows me to see it more clearly and aligns with other parts of my understanding. Once you have applied your discernment

---

3. ibid

and begun to incorporate the practices into your daily life, a cleaner, more congruent fit will emerge. As we journey and mature, through our psychological and spiritual filters, we strive to maintain an open acceptance of this process for ourselves and others, continuing to grow and avoid grasping and clinging to fundamentalist positions.

About the Author

Doug Henning lives with his wife Joyce of 60 years in Parker, Colorado. The couple has two sons and six grandchildren. He is a Vietnam War veteran. He has a Bachelor's Degree in Corrective Therapy and a Master's Degree in Psychology from Pacific Lutheran University in Tacoma, Washington. His PhD is from Oregon State University. Doug completed an Internship in Sexual Dysfunction in the Adult Development program at the University of Washington in Seattle, did a Clinical Fellowship in Rehabilitation Psychology at The Rehabilitation Institute in Kansas City, Missouri, and completed a graduate Certificate in Cross-Cultural Ministry at Nazarene Theological Seminary in Kansas City, Missouri. He has held professional licenses to Practice Psychology in Washington State, Kansas, Missouri, and Colorado.

Acknowledgements

Much thanks to SacraSage publications for their willingness to publish my work. Specific thanks to Jonathan Foster.

I'm also so very grateful to the gentle Thai people, who, by virtue of *being*, allowed me to live in their country in 1969 and to be introduced to their culture and religion of Buddhism. I could have never imagined the impact you would have on me over the last nearly 60 years.

And of course, to Joyce, who immediately swept me off my feet in February 1965. I love you!

www.ingramcontent.com/pod-product-compliance
Lightning Source LLC
Chambersburg PA
CBHW021323060726
47591CB00006B/1845